Olympiad ACE

A Comprehensive Practice Book

for School Olympiads & Talent Search Exams

ENGLISH

Class 9

BLOOM

Olympiad ACE

A Comprehensive Practice Book

for School Olympiads & Talent Search Exams

ENGLISH

Class 9

by

Vaishali Jaiswal

BLOOM
Bloom Cap Edu Ventures Pvt. Ltd.

卐 **Administrative & Production Office**

'Ramchhaya' 4577/15, Agarwal Road, Darya Ganj, New Delhi -110002
Tele: 011- 47630600, 43518550

卐 **PRICE:** ₹125.00

卐 **PO No :** TXT-59-T066823-08-25

Published by Arihant Publications (I) Ltd.

For further information about the books log on to
www.bloomcap.org

Follow us on

Preface

"Future belongs to those Who prepares for it today"

School Olympiads are National & International level competitions conducted by different Government, Non-Government & Educational Organisations with the purpose of making the children ready to face competitive exams.

The challenging Questions asked in Olympiads motivate them to learn more & more and bring out the best results with improved academic performance. The Awards & Scholarship offered by Olympiads motivate children to aspire & strive for doing better and emerge out to be the best.

English Olympiads

English is one of the most widely spoken languages across the world. In today's era, good command over English is considered as a must have skill. The greatest advantage of studying English is improvement in communication skills along with the growth of personality.

English Olympiads are meant to strengthen students' command over this universal language by improving spellings, grammar, sentence structure and to master student's language skills.

'Bloom English Olympiad Study Book Class 9' is a perfect resource to Study & Practice for Olympiad Exams and other National & State Level Talent Search Exams & Other Competitions.

Some Special Features of Bloom English Olympiad Study Books are;

- Complete coverage of all the aspects of English; Grammar, Reading Comprehension, Writing Skills, Spellings, Vocabulary & Communication Skills.
- Chapterwise Exercises having different types of Objective Questions at par with the Olympiad Level.
- Olympiad Pattern Practice Sets at the end.

This book is prepared by Expert Panel with the utmost care, still if you have any suggestions regarding its improvement then feel free to contact us at support@bloomcap.org. We will try to inculcate your suggestions in the further editions.

Contents

Chapter 01

Parts of Speech

1 Mark Questions

Directions (Q. Nos. 1-3) Identify the type of noun of the underlined words.

1. A suicide attack on a foreign military <u>convey</u> in Afghanistan killed 11 children.
(a) Proper noun
(b) Abstract noun
(c) Collective noun
(d) Material noun

2. He should get an award for <u>bravery</u>.
(a) Collective noun
(b) Proper noun
(c) Common noun
(d) Abstract noun

3. Which of the following is not an abstract noun?
(a) Goodness (b) Family
(c) Bravery (d) Childhood

Directions (Q. Nos. 4-6) Change the words given in brackets to nouns and complete the sentences.

4. The .... (place) of the matter in the text was not appropriate.
(a) placement
(b) placing
(c) placed
(d) places

5. You do not have the .... (authorise) to take action against this.
(a) authoritarian (b) author
(c) authority (d) None of these

6. He left the house with some of his .... (belong).
(a) belongs (b) belonged
(c) belonging (d) belongings

7. Select the option with incorrect plural form.
(a) Hawks (b) Rattlers
(c) Skys (d) Enemies

8. Select the option with incorrect plural form.
(a) Coyotes (b) Ashes
(c) Medicines (d) Decoyes

Directions (Q. Nos. 9 and 10) Fill in the blanks with suitable feminine forms of the noun.

9. He is a famous actor. His mother was also a famous .... of her times.
(a) heroine (b) actress
(c) protagonist (d) writer

10. He bought a beautiful chestnut horse but he actually wanted to buy a ....
(a) fowl (b) neigh
(c) mare (d) lass

Directions (Q. Nos. 11-15) Choose the correct sentence from the options given below.

11. (a) All the news were sad.
(b) All newses were sad.
(c) All the news was sad.
(d) Every news were sad.

12. (a) Richard gifted her three gold jewellery.
(b) Richard gifted her three gold jewelleries.
(c) Richard gifted her three items of gold jewellery.
(d) Richard gifted her three items of gold jewelleries.

13. (a) The people of India are peace loving.
(b) The people of India is peace loving.
(c) The peoples of India are peace loving.
(d) The peoples of India is peace loving.

14. (a) Riya has four pencil.
(b) Riya has four sticks of pencil.
(c) Riya has four sticks of pencils.
(d) Riya has four pencils.

15. (a) You need a lots of patience.
(b) You needs a lot of patience.
(c) You need a lot of patience.
(d) You need a lot of patiences.

Directions (Q. Nos. 16-20) Fill in the blanks with the appropriate options given below.

16. She spread .... on the table but left the .... because there were many flies in them.
(a) cupses, dishes (b) cups, dish
(c) cup, dishes (d) cups, dishes

17. The doctors have tried many .... to kill the harmful ....
(a) formulas, bacterium
(b) formulae, bacteria
(c) formulae, bacterias
(d) formulas, bacteria

18. The .... took away all things kept on the .... They cut many things into .... with the ....
(a) thiefs, shelves, half, knives
(b) thieves, shelves, halves, knives
(c) thieves, shelf, half, knife
(d) thief, shelves, half, knives

19. The ....that this firm supplies good .... and .... proved wrong.
(a) informations, furnitures, stationaries
(b) information, furniture, stationery
(c) information, furnitures, stationries
(d) information, furnitures, stationery

20. The students drew their own .... and included them in their ....
There are no ...... for such ....
(a) hypotheses, synopses, criteria, phenomena
(b) hypothesises, synopsises, criterions, phenomenons
(c) hypothesis, synopsis, criteria, phenomenon
(d) hypothesis, synopsis, criterion, phenomena

Directions (Q. Nos. 21-27) Fill in the blanks with suitable pronouns.

21. Somebody stole my wallet yesterday. .... took it from my desk.
(a) He (b) She
(c) Those (d) They

22. He is older than .... so I have to respect and give priority to ....
(a) myself/himself (b) mine/his
(c) me/his (d) me/him

23. He imagined all of the possibilities about the place .... he lost his wallet. .... was only the post-office that he hadn't looked for his lost things.
(a) that/These (b) in which/This
(c) whom/Here (d) where/There

24. Isn't it all plain that it is all these lacks that make Queen Victoria so old fashioned, so finally and awfully different from ...., rather than the fact that .... never flew in an airplane or had a hydrogen bomb dropped on ....?

(a) us/she/her (b) them/her/us
(c) them/she/us (d) him/his/him

25. We all remember that Queen Victoria, when .... died in 1901, had never got to see a helicopter, a television set, penicillin, an electric refrigerator. Yet .... had seen railroads, electric lights. .... came about midway in the industrial revolution that has transformed .... world.

(a) she/she/Her/her (b) she/her/She/her
(c) she/she/She/our (d) she/she/Her/out

26. When Disraeli and Gladstone made speeches for Queen Victoria's government, the speeches weren't written for .... by ghost writers. When ...... sent .... lovingly or respectfully inscribed copies of .... new books, ... had written the books themselves.

(a) them/they/her/their/they
(b) her/they/their/her/they
(c) her/they/their/their/she
(d) them/she/her/her/she

27. Everyone was upset by the mysterious stranger. No one knew .... he had come or .... he was going to do.

(a) which/when (b) that/how
(c) who/whom (d) why/what

28. Which is the relative pronoun in the sentence?
"That was the boy whom I saw in the party last night."

(a) That (b) I
(c) Whom (d) Them

29. Which is the distributive pronoun in the sentence?
"Each of the boy in my class knows how to keep discipline in the class."

(a) My (b) How
(c) Each (d) The

30. Which is the indefinite pronoun in the sentence?
"Someone called the firefighter, when the house was on fire."

(a) Someone (b) When
(c) Was (d) On

31. A baby learns the meaning of words as ...... are spoken by others and later uses ...... in sentences.

(a) their/they (b) they/them
(c) they/themselves (d) they/it

32. Some of these clothes are ....., and the rest of .... belong to Zack.

(a) yours/it
(b) my/them
(c) hers/their
(d) mine/them

Directions (Q. Nos. 33-37) Read the following passage carefully. Fill in the blanks with correct forms of verb.

Coffee is a beverage ...**(33)**... (drink) by many past generations of people. What most people do not realise is that coffee is ...**(34)**... (make) from beans ...**(35)**... (pick) from trees. Coffee trees ...**(36)**... (grow) either from seeds or cuttings. These trees will begin to ...**(37)**... (bear) crops when they are about four years old.

33. (a) drinks (b) drunk
(c) has drunk (d) had drunk

34. (a) make (b) being made
(c) made (d) making

35. (a) picked (b) picks
(c) being picked (d) were picked

36. (a) grows (b) grown
(c) are growing (d) are grown

37. (a) bearing (b) will bear
(c) bear (d) bore

Directions (Q. Nos. 38-43) Fill in the blanks with suitable options.

38. I .... for a pen .... this composition.
(a) look, write
(b) am looking, to write
(c) look, for writing
(d) have been looking, for writing

39. She .... up the stairs slowly because she didn't want ....
(a) was climbing, fall
(b) climbed, to fall
(c) was climbing, falling
(d) had climbed, to be fallen

40. The teacher .... the students .... the sum.
(a) was asking, to solve
(b) asked, solved
(c) asked, to solve
(d) has asked, for solve

41. Nobody .... that he is innocent.
(a) is believing (b) believes
(c) believe (d) believed

42. Although the children were tired, they .... playing.
(a) were continuing
(b) continued
(c) are continuing
(d) had continued

43. The stranger .... the shopkeeper to give him a glass of water because he .... thirsty.
(a) was requesting, was
(b) requested, was
(c) requested, is
(d) has requested, was

Directions (Q. Nos. 44-46) For each of the following sentences, choose the correct order of adjectives to fill in the blanks.

44. His grandfather lives in the .... house down the street.
(a) big old yellow (b) yellow old big
(c) old big yellow (d) big yellow old

45. The shop offers all kinds of ...... objects.
(a) interesting old antique
(b) old antique interesting
(c) old interesting antique
(d) interesting antique old

46. We went for a long walk on a .... trail.
(a) beautiful, new 5-mile
(b) new, beautiful 5-mile
(c) 5-mile, new, beautiful
(d) new-5-mile, beautiful

Directions (Q. Nos. 47-54) Complete the following sentences by choosing the right option.

47. The ballon got .... and bigger.
(a) bigger (b) big
(c) biggest (d) more big

48. He had only .... mangoes.
(a) a little (b) many
(c) five (d) fewer

49. The lockdown has been lifted so I am feding .... now.
(a) happier (b) happy
(c) happiest (d) more happy

50. He had lost .... his wealth.
(a) entire (b) whole
(c) all (d) less

51. The faster you drive, the .... it is.
(a) more dangerous (b) dangerous
(c) most dangerous (d) very dangerous

52. He saw it with his ...... eyes.
(a) owned (b) owner
(c) own (d) our

53. He was a man of ...... ambition.
(a) greatest (b) greater
(c) great (d) greed

54. Sonali's marks are the .... in the class.
(a) high
(b) higher
(c) highest
(d) None of the above

Directions (Q. Nos. 55-58) Fill in the blanks by choosing the appropriate adverbs.

55. I have heard this ....
(a) now (b) before
(c) never (d) since

56. I have told you ......
(a) never (b) twice
(c) seldom (d) fully

57. This story is written........
(a) surely (b) certainly
(c) well (d) once

58. She sings ....
(a) delighted (b) delightfully
(c) already (d) never

Directions (Q. Nos. 59-62) Choose the correct sentence.

59. (a) Jim never is at work.
(b) Jim is at work never.
(c) Never is Jim at work.
(d) Jim is never at work.

60. (a) We have usually lunch at 12 o'clock.
(b) We usually have lunch at 12 o'clock.
(c) We have lunch at usually 12 o'clock.
(d) We have lunch at 12 usually o'clock.

61. (a) She travels always by train.
(b) Always she travels by train.
(c) She always travels by train.
(d) She travels by always train.

62. (a) They go out sometimes in the evening.
(b) They sometimes go out in the evening.
(c) They go out in sometimes the evening.
(d) They go sometimes out in the evening.

Directions (Q. Nos. 63-65) Fill in the blanks with suitable options.

63. Come here .... You have to see this!
(a) quietly (b) quickly
(c) beautifully (d) carelessly

64. We knew that she had got the job when we saw her talking .... on the phone.
(a) carefully (b) slowly
(c) excitedly (d) finally

65. He ...... put the vase on the table. It fell to the floor.
(a) carefully
(b) carelessly
(c) beautifully
(d) loudly

Directions (Q. Nos. 66-70) Fill in the blanks by choosing the correct options.

66. .... member is allowed to bring a guest.
(a) Every (b) Each
(c) All (d) None of these

67. .... ice cream shop has ..... flowers imaginable.
(a) This, all (b) That, every
(c) Each, all (d) Those, all

68. Last summer we went on .... cruise in the Caribbean. Among .... islands we visited were Bermuda and Bahamas.
(a) -/the (b) a/the
(c) the/an (d) the/-

69. .... Amazon in Brazil is ...... longest river.
(a) The/the
(b) A/the
(c) An/the
(d) The/a

70. The report concludes sadly that ...... students have .... knowledge of nuclear physics.
(a) some/lot of (b) all/little
(c) both/whole (d) None of these

2 Marks Questions

Directions (Q. Nos. 71-75) Fill in the blanks with the correct preposition. Choose the correct option for each sentence.

71. The first McDonald's restaurant was opened ...... Dick and Mac McDonald ...... the 15th ...... May 1940.
(a) on, of, with
(b) by, on, in
(c) by, on, of
(d) with, on, in

72. The best selling products .... their restaurant were hamburgers.
(a) on (b) of
(c) at (d) in

73. So, the McDonald brothers thought .... a way to produce hamburgers more quickly.
(a) about (b) of
(c) over (d) with

74. This was introduced .... 1948 and became known as the speeder service system.
(a) on (b) in
(c) at (d) about

75. The first franchised McDonald's restaurant was opened ...... 1953 and today you can find McDonald's restaurants .... more than 100 Countries.
(a) on, in (b) at, in
(c) in, in (d) about, in

Directions (Q. Nos. 76-80) Complete the following sentences by choosing suitable connectors from the given options.

76. I think you'll like her, I should .... warn you, that she is quite eccentric, ... she is a terrible cook and her dinners are inedible.
(a) so that, but also
(b) however, moreover
(c) therefore, nevertheless
(d) but, and

77. I'm not going to make a long speech .... I know we all want to go home. .... my English is not so good that I can speak for hours.
(a) but, For anything
(b) so that, However
(c) moreover, However
(d) as, Moreover

78. I should be delighted to attend the Seminar. .... all expenses are borne by you. I will need a confirmation soon, ... I can make necessary travel arrangements.
(a) Provided that, so that
(b) In case, as
(c) even if, so
(d) however, so

79. India really didn't expect to win. ...., they were disappointed at their poor performance.
(a) However (b) Even though
(c) Despite (d) Nevertheless

80. Her, husband lost his job. .... she decided to take up a job ...... her baby was just a year old.

(a) So that, even if
(b) Therefore, even though
(c) However, but
(d) Therefore, but

Directions (Q.Nos. 81-90) Identify the errors related to parts of speech. If there is no error, mark your answer as 'd'.

81. There are so much filths (a)/all around (b)/ the place. (c)/ No error (d)

82. The sceneries (a)/ of Kashmir (b)/ is very charming. (c)/ No error (d)

83. You and I (a)/ have done (b)/ my best in the examination. (c)/ No error (d)

84. If somcone has (a)/finished the work (b)/ he may go home. (c)/ No error (d)

85. The whole block of flats (a)/ including two shops (b)/ was destroyed in fire. (c)/No error (d)

86. In most of the states (a)/forty per cent of people under thirty years (b)/ is undernourished. (c)/ No error (d)

87. The Railways have made (a)/ crossing the tracks (b)/ a punished offence. (c)/ No error (d)

88. Anish is clever (a)/ than any other (b)/ person in this company. (c)/ No error (d)

89. No sooner (a)/ I had spoken (b)/ than he left. (c)/ No error (d)

90. Is the room (a)/ enough large to (b)/ accommodate twenty boys of our school. (c)/ No error (d)

Chapter

02

Subject-Verb Agreement

1 Mark Questions

Directions (Q. Nos. 1-6) Fill in the blanks with the correct form of verb in the following sentence.

1. 'Northern Lights' .... one of Suzanne's favourite books.

(a) are (b) is
(c) was (d) have

2. .... effort is required for financial planning.

(a) A lots of
(b) A lot of
(c) A number of
(d) Something

3. A number of apartment blocks here .... their own swimming pool.

(a) are (b) has
(c) have (d) had

4. Dr Jone's whereabouts .... kept a closely guarded secret by his friend.

(a) are
(b) was
(c) is
(d) has been

5. .... somebody taken my note book? I can't find it anywhere.

(a) Has (b) Have
(c) Is (d) Was

6. Bad weather on public holidays .... people from going out.

(a) discouraged
(b) discourages
(c) discourage
(d) is discouraging

Directions (Q. Nos. 7-11) Fill in the blanks with suitable form of verb.

7. There........... a moment of silence to honour all those who had given their lives for the action.

(a) is (b) was (c) are (d) were

8. The power of ruling party .... by a popular opposition party.

(a) was challenged (b) were challenged
(c) has challenged (d) are challenged

9. John's ability to read other people's mind .... truly amazing.

(a) are (b) were
(c) is (d) has

10. Gratitude .... conveyed to all those who donated to the charity.

(a) have been (b) are being
(c) will (d) has been

11. Approval for the playground projects .... granted by the city council.

(a) has been (b) have been
(c) will (d) is

Directions (Q. Nos. 12-18) In each of following sentences choose the correct form of verb according to the subject. Choose from the options to fill the gap.

12. An astrologer, as my friends tell me, ... events or developments.
(a) predicts (b) predicted
(c) predict (d) is predicting

13. The person together with three other saints .... to make a number of startling predictions.
(a) plans (b) plan
(c) is planning (d) has planned

14. These predictions .... not to be believed.
(a) was (b) were (c) is (d) are

15. My sister, along with her husband and my parents .... driving to a wedding this weekend.
(a) is (b) are (c) was (d) were

16. Inside my fridge .... a can of diet Pepsi and a piece of old cake.
(a) are (b) is
(c) was (d) were

17. One of my brothers .... in Atlanta last weekend.
(a) was (b) are
(c) were (d) is

18. The teacher as well as her students .... that practise makes a man perfect.
(a) are believing (b) believes
(c) believe (d) believed

Directions (Q. Nos. 19-28) Choose the correct option to complete the sentence.

19. Either the physicians in this hospital or Chief administrator .... going to make a decision.
(a) is (b) are
(c) was (d) were

20. .... my boss or my sisters in the union going to win this grievance?
(a) is (b) are
(c) has (d) have

21. Some of the votes .... to have been miscounted.
(a) seems (b) seem
(c) seemed (d) has seemed

22. The tornadoes that tear through this country every year .... more than just a nuisance.
(a) are (b) was
(c) were (d) is

23. Everyone selected to serve on this jury .... to be willing to give up a lot of time.
(a) have (b) had
(c) has (d) are

24. Shivani Wangu together with her teammates, ... a formidable opponent on the cricket ground.
(a) present (b) presents
(c) presenting (d) have presented

25. He seems to forget that there .... things to be done before he can graduate.
(a) is (b) are
(c) were (d) was

26. Some people .... still left in the town after yesterday's earthquake.
(a) is (b) were
(c) are (d) was

27. Some of the grain .... to be contaminated.
(a) appears (b) appeared
(c) have appeared (d) appear

28. Three quarters of the students .... against the tuition hike.

(a) were (b) is
(c) are (d) was

Directions (Q. Nos. 29-35) Fill in the most appropriate verb so that it agrees with the subject.

29. Later that evening our luggage .... at last found and returned to us.

(a) was (b) were
(c) has (d) have been

30. Who .... seen this film before?

(a) have (b) has
(c) had (d) was

31. There .... lots of news to tell you.

(a) is (b) are
(c) was (d) were

32. One in two people .... received wrongly delivered mail in the last six months.

(a) has (b) have
(c) had (d) have been

33. A number of residents .... complained about the noise.

(a) are (b) was
(c) has (d) have

34. I am looking for really juicy items of news. Trivia .... not interest me.

(a) do (b) does
(c) are (d) is

35. Five times five .... twenty five.

(a) is (b) are
(c) was (d) were

Directions (Q. Nos. 36-40) Fill in the blanks with suitable options.

36. One of my earrings .... disappeared.

(a) have (b) has
(c) is (d) are

37. A lot of children never .... the computer at the weekend.

(a) will leave (b) has left
(c) leave (d) leaves

38. A number of items .... been dealt with yet.

(a) hasn't been (b) haven't been
(c) aren't (d) isn't

39. The team of rescuers .... working round the clock.

(a) is (b) are (c) has (d) had

40. Every new class of pupils .... a new challange, says one teacher.

(a) has (b) had (c) are (d) is

2 Marks Questions

41. Replace the underlined word with correct verb.

Besides encountering the strange aborigines, the first English settlers <u>had find</u> (i) in the presence of new and wide variations of climate. In their old home, they <u>were accustomed</u> (ii) to a moderate temperature. Now they <u>have</u> (iii) before them a great range of climate from the cold coasts to hot savannahs.

(i) (a) find (b) found
(c) have found (d) will find

(ii) (a) was accustomed
(b) have been accustomed
(c) had been accustomed
(d) are accustomed

(iii) (a) had
(b) has had
(c) have had
(d) will have

42. Replace the underlined word with correct verb.

To the exigencies of these variations, all the immigrants from the British isles as well as the continent <u>have</u> (i) to adapt themselves. Wherever the colonists set to work they <u>braved</u> (ii) hostile weather conditions.

(i) (a) have had (b) will have
(c) had (d) had been

(ii) (a) will brave
(b) are braving
(c) will be braving
(d) were braving

43. Choose the correct options.

1. Each of these producers has his own advantage.
2. Ten miles are a long distance.
3. Either boys or girls are telling lies.

Which of the above sentence are correct?

Codes

(a) 1 and 2 (b) 2 and 3
(c) 1 and 3 (d) 1, 2 and 3

44. Choose the correct options.

1. The furniture in his house look expensive.
2. Most of my friends is government employees.
3. The fort stand in the middle of the Thar desert.

Which of the above statements is correct?

Codes

(a) 1 and 2 (b) 1 and 3
(c) 1, 2 and 3 (d) None of these

45. Choose the correct options.

Although every student in the class .... the schedule, one of my students always .... late to the class.

(a) know, come (b) knows, coming
(c) knows, comes (d) knows, came

46. Choose the correct options.

Only when each of the committee members .... reading the instructions then can you .... them to the hall.

(a) would finish/took
(b) is finishing/be taking
(c) finishes/take
(d) finished/ take

47. Match the following.

List I	List II	List II
(i) Either Hasan or Hamid	A. were	1. about the schedule
(ii) He and I	B. have been confused	2. to the meeting
(iii) Students' minds	C. is coming	3. good friends

Codes

(a) (i)-A-1, (ii)-B-2, (iii)-C-3
(b) (i)-B-2, (ii)-C-1, (iii)-A-3
(c) (i)-C-3, (ii)-B-1, (iii)-A-2
(d) (i)-C-2, (ii)-A-3, (iii)-B-1

Chapter 03

Tenses

1 Mark Questions

Directions (Q. Nos. 1-5) Choose the correct verb forms to complete the sentences.

1. In the last decade, there .... a significant breakthrough in the treatment of some terminal illnesses.

(a) has been
(b) was
(c) had been
(d) will have been

2. Since I changed the job I .... more time to relax and enjoy my hobbies.

(a) found
(b) have found
(c) will find
(d) have been finding

3. She .... a house from her father who died last May.

(a) has inherited
(b) inherited
(c) had inherited
(d) has had inherited

4. Poverty today .... some parents to leave their families.

(a) forced
(b) has forced
(c) will have been forced
(d) forces

5. In the last hundred years man .... great advances in the fields of science and technology.

(a) achieved
(b) has achieved
(c) had achieved
(d) has been achieving

Directions (Q. Nos. 6-10) Five friends have just finished some job. Look at the table. Complete the dialogues from this information using the appropriate tense.

		Activity	Now
Arti	⟶	Sweep the floors	She is Sweating.
Aman	⟶	Cut the grass	He is tired.
Paul	⟶	Do the washing up	He has soft hands.
Tarun	⟶	Peel the onions	He has red eyes.
Meena	⟶	Defrost the fridge	He has cold hands.

6. Arti why are you sweating? Because I ....

(a) have been sweeping the floors
(b) have been washing the dishes
(c) have been cutting the grass
(d) has been peeling the onions

7. Is the lawn finished? Yes Aman ....
(a) Aman had cut the grass
(b) Aman has cut the grass
(c) Aman has been cutting the grass
(d) Aman cut the grass

8. Paul, why are your hands so soft? Because I ....
(a) have done the washing
(b) have done the cutting
(c) have done the sweeping
(d) have done the cooking

9. Why are your eyes red Tarun? Because ....
(a) I was cutting the onions
(b) I have been cutting the onions
(c) I cut the onions
(d) I will have cut the onions

10. Is the fridge all right now? Yes ....
(a) Meena had defrosted the fridge
(b) Meena defrosted the fridge
(c) Meena has defrosted the fridge
(d) Meena will defrost the fridge.

Directions (Q. Nos. 11-16) Choose the correct tense form to fill the blanks.

11. If people of different backgrounds .... to live in harmony, we would have a happier society.
(a) had learned
(b) is learning
(c) learned
(d) have learnt

12. I wish I .... more organised and meticulous in my work.
(a) was
(b) am
(c) were
(d) will

13. The importance of genetic engineering .... changes to the genes of a plant or an animal.
(a) are making (b) has made
(c) is making (d) will be making

14. A number of .... that eating organic produce has health benefits.
(a) study shows
(b) study show
(c) studies show
(d) study are showing

15. Few people .... the use of GM ingredients earlier. But it has increased dramatically in recent years.
(a) have been aware of
(b) are aware of
(c) were aware of
(d) was aware of

16. People .... creating meat in laboratories for several years now.
(a) are (b) have been
(c) is/was (d) will

Directions (Q. Nos. 17-25) Fill in the blanks with suitable verbs (use simple past or past continuous tense).

It ......**(17)**..... (be) another escapade of Gopi and Gargi into the forest. The two ......**(18)**...... (play) in the courtyard of the ruined castle when they ......**(19)**...... (hear) strange sounds as if someone ......**(20)**....... (ring) tiny bells in a temple. But there was none in the vicinity. They ......**(21)**...... (know) it. Then who ......**(22)**...... (make) those sounds? Nothing of that sort had happened during any of their earlier visits. Was the castle ......**(23)**...... (haunt)? Suddenly this thought ......**(24)**.....(have) a vice like grip on their minds. Both were terrified but neither ......**(25)**....... (want) to admit it.

Options

17. (a) is (b) were
(c) was (d) has been

18. (a) has been playing (b) were playing
(c) was playing (d) is playing

19. (a) heard (b) had heard
(c) have heard (d) hearing

20. (a) will be ringing (b) was ringing
(c) were ringing (d) ringing

21. (a) have known (b) had known
(c) knew (d) has known

22. (a) was making (b) has been making
(c) made (d) were making

23. (a) was haunting
(b) haunted
(c) has been haunting
(d) had haunted

24. (a) is having (b) has
(c) had (d) have

25. (a) was wanting
(b) wanted
(c) has been wanting
(d) were wanting

Directions (Q. Nos. 26-30) A paragraph is given, where some sentences have been underlined and numbered. Identify the type of tense for each sentence by choosing from the options.

NAREDCO has convened a two-day conclave **26.** involving all the stakeholders of the real estate industry—Union Ministers, department secretaries, CMs, developers, officials of banks and financial institutions, etc—to discuss the strategy for implementing 'Housing for all by 2022'.

Prabhakar Sinha writes **27.** In order to capitalise upon the opportunity offered by Prime Minister Narendra Modi's ambitious plan of 'Housing for all by 2022', real estate developers are convening a series **28.** of meetings with states and central ministers, decision makers and government officials.

This augurs well for the **29.** real estate sector as whole and is likely to be a major factor in reviving the economy.

The topics for discussion in the meeting include speedy clearances, **30.** standardisation and simplification of procedures involving aviation, environment, administrative bottlenecks, land acquisition, non-agricultural conversion, affordable housing through Public Private Participation (PPP), legal issues, urban planning, technologies and innovation for creating new cities and issues related to SEZ and reforms.

26. (a) Present perfect (b) Past perfect
(c) Present simple (d) Past simple

27. (a) Simple past
(b) Present continuous
(c) Simple present
(d) Simple future

28. (a) Past continuous
(b) Present continuous
(c) Future continuous
(d) Simple future

29. (a) Simple future
(b) Simple past
(c) Simple present
(d) Past perfect

30. (a) Simple present
(b) Simple past
(c) Simple future
(d) Present continuous

Directions (Q. Nos. 31-36) Fill in the blanks by choosing the correct option.

31. Early signs of the rebirth of civilisation in Western Europe .... to appear in the 11th century as trade .... again in Italy.

(a) were beginning/will start
(b) began/started
(c) would begin/starts
(d) began/would be starting

32. When a group .... to a new country, its members .... that they have to modify their way of life, including their celebrations of significant events.

(a) will immigrate/find
(b) immigrated/would find
(c) immigrates/find
(d) were immigrating/found

33. When he .... that his nomination would mean competing with his closest friend he .... to with draw.

(a) realises/will be decided
(b) realise/was deciding
(c) will realise/decides
(d) realised/decided

34. The immune system .... by distinguishing between the body's own materials and things that .... foreign to the body.

(a) is working/were
(b) works/would be
(c) will be working/are
(d) works/are

35. .... seen Kate recently? She .... another baby.

(a) Did you/was going to have
(b) Has you/was going to have
(c) Have you/is going to have
(d) Is any one/will have

36. As soon as there .... even a temporary break in the weather, the climbers .... their attempt to reach the summit.

(a) is/will renew
(b) was/renew
(c) will be/renewed
(d) is/renewed

2 Marks Questions

Directions (Q. Nos. 37 and 38) Replace the underlined word with suitable form of verb from the options given below.

37. Since (i) the past two years I am studying (ii) English. I knew a little English before I came here, but my English has improve (iii) a lot.

(i) (a) For (b) During (c) From (d) Till
(ii) (a) was studying (b) will be studying (c) have been studying (d) have studied
(iii) (a) improved (b) had been improving (c) had improved (d) has improved

38. I start (i) to work in a factory three months ago. Since I start (ii) my job, I haven't have (iii)much time for fun.

(i) (a) have started (b) started (c) am starting (d) will start
(ii) (a) starting (b) have started (c) started (d) have been started
(iii) (a) did not have (b) hadn't have (c) am not having (d) haven't' had

39. Choose the correct option.

1. Just as I was leaving the house, the phone rang.
2. Prices of petrol will rise again next year.
3. I have been making this dress for last friday.

Which of the above sentences are correct?

(a) 1 and 2 (b) 2 and 3
(c) 1 and 3 (d) 1, 2 and 3

40. Choose the correct option.

1. I was walking with the dog tomorrow morning.
2. I would have been sleeping yesterday.
3. The results have just been announced.

Which of the above sentences is correct?

(a) Only 1 (b) Only 2
(c) Only 3 (d) None of these

41. Change the tense of the verbs as directed.

He was distributing newspapers to the entire neighbourhood (Change to Simple Present)

A. He is distributing newpapers to the entire neighbourhood.
B. He distribute newpapers to the entire neighbourhood.
D. He distributed newpapers to the entire neighbourhood.
D. He distributes newpapers to the entire neighbourhood.

Codes

(a) Only A (b) Both A and C
(c) Only D (d) A, B and C

42. Change the tense of the verbs as directed.

We will visit our cousins during holiday. (Change to Simple Past)

A. We visited our cousins during holidays.
B. We had visited our cousins during holidays.
C. We would have visited our cousins during holidays.
D. We were visiting our cousins during holidays.

Codes

(a) Only B (b) Only A
(c) A, B and C (d) B, C and D

43. Match the following.

List I	List II	List II
(i) The lesson	A. left	1. for two hours when he arrived
(ii) We	B. had begun	2. home a week ago
(iii) Eva	C. had been waiting	3. when we arrived

Codes

(a) (i)-A-1, (ii)-B-2, (iii)-C-3
(b) (i)-B-1, (ii)-C-3, (iii)-A-2
(c) (i)-B-3, (ii)-C-1, (iii)-A-2
(d) (i)-A-2, (ii)-B-3, (iii)-C-1

Chapter 04

Clauses and Conditionals

1 Mark Questions

Directions (Q. Nos. 1-15) Fill in the blanks(s) with suitable option.

1. If I had enough money, I .... that radio.

(a) bought
(b) would buy
(c) would have bought
(d) had bought

2. If it rains, you .... wet.

(a) will get (b) would get
(c) got (d) had got

3. She would go to the Job Centre if she .... a job.

(a) had wanted (b) will want
(c) wanted (d) wants

4. The dog .... you if it hadn't been tied up.

(a) would bite
(b) will bite
(c) would have bitten
(d) bites

5. It .... easy to paint pictures if you knew how to.

(a) would be
(b) had been
(c) would have been
(d) be

6. If I come, I .... you.

(a) saw (b) would see
(c) will see (d) sees

7. She .... pleased if you came.

(a) would be
(b) would have been
(c) would has been
(d) was

8. If it .... I would stay at home.

(a) rains (b) rained
(c) has rained (d) had rained

9. You will catch the train if you .... earlier.

(a) left (b) leaves
(c) leave (d) would leave

10. If he .... thirsty, he would have drunk some water.

(a) was (b) had been
(c) is (d) would

11. If I .... to Leipzig, I'll visit the zoo.

(a) go (b) went
(c) had gone (d) will go

12. If it .... , we'd be in the garden.

(a) doesn't rain
(b) didn't rain
(c) won't rain
(d) hadn't rained

13. If you .... a lighter jacket, the car driver would have seen you earlier.
(a) wear
(b) had been wearing
(c) wore
(d) had worn

14. We .... TV tonight if Peter hadn't bought the theatre tickets.
(a) will watch
(b) would watch
(c) would have watched
(d) were watching

15. She wouldn't have had two laptops if she .... one to her friend.
(a) does not lend
(b) did not lend
(c) had not lent
(d) lent

Directions (Q. Nos. 16-22) Fill in the blank(s) with suitable options.

16. If you .... to bed earlier yesterday you .... late now.
(a) had gone/ wouldn't get up
(b) went/ wouldn't have got up
(c) had gone/ wouldn't have got up
(d) went/ wouldn't get up

17. If the democratic alternative to the totalitarian one-way broadcasts .... a row of separate soap boxes, then I .... that the alternative .... unworkable.
(a) is / submit/ is
(b) were/ submit/ would have been
(c) had been/ had submit/ would be
(d) is/ would submit/ will be

18. If I .... a rich man, I .... that car.
(a) was/ will buy
(b) had been / would buy
(c) were/ would buy
(d) had been / will buy

19. If I .... enough money yesterday I .... that shirt.
(a) had/ would buy
(b) had/ would have bought
(c) have/ will buy
(d) have had/ will be able to buy

20. Had you brought your umbrella, you .... so wet yesterday evening.
(a) wouldn't have been
(b) will be
(c) won't be
(d) weren't going to be

21. If you .... them to your birthday party last month, they ....
(a) had invited/ may come
(b) have invited/ might have come
(c) invited/ would come
(d) had invited / might have come

22. If I .... in your shoes yesterday, I .... her that she should deal with her problems herself.
(a) were/ would tell
(b) was/ would tell
(c) had been / would have told
(d) am / will tell

Directions (Q. Nos. 23-30) Fill in the blanks with suitable options.

23. Do you think there would be less conflict in the world if all people .... the same language?
(a) will speak (b) speak
(c) had spoken (d) spoke

24. If you can give me one good reason for your acting like this, ... this incident again.
(a) I will never mention
(b) I never mention
(c) will I never mention
(d) I don't mention

25. Unless you .... all of my questions, I can't do anything to help you.

(a) answered
(b) answer
(c) would answer
(d) were answering

26. Had you told me that this was going to happen, I .... it.

(a) would never have believed
(b) hadn't believed
(c) don't believe
(d) can't believe

27. .... we truly understand others can we show sympathy towards them.

(a) Only if
(b) Unless
(c) Even if
(d) But for

28. My parents have been my emotional safety net and I .... the hardships in life without their constant support and attention.

(a) didn't survive
(b) wouldn't have survived
(c) haven't survived
(d) hadn't survived

29. If I were in your shoes, I think I .... to her rather than try to explain what has happened over the phone.

(a) spoke (b) have spoken
(c) would speak (d) will speak

30. If I .... the consequences of my action, I would not have acted so hastily.

(a) have realised (b) realise
(c) realised (d) had realised

2 Marks Questions

31. Match the 'if clauses' given in List-I to their main clauses given in List-II.

List-I	List-II
A. If Steven goes out,	1. he will get fat.
B. If Jack was at school today,	2. it would not smell in our room.
C. If Steven eats so many sweets	3. he'll never take an umbrella with him.
D. If Jack washed his feet	4. he would know about the history test.

Codes

	A	B	C	D
(a)	1	2	3	4
(b)	3	4	2	1
(c)	3	4	1	2
(d)	2	1	4	3

32. Match the 'if clauses' given in List-I to their main clauses given in List-II.

List-I	List-II
A. If Rahul didn't foul the other players as often,	1. he can save more money.
B. If Jayesh read the newspaper regularly,	2. he could be better at current affairs.
C. If Shreya didn't play the music too loud,	3. her neighbour would not be angry with her.
D. If Rohan turns off the heating more often,	4. he would be in the school team.

Codes

	A	B	C	D		A	B	C	D
(a)	1	2	3	4	(b)	4	2	3	1
(c)	3	4	1	2	(d)	2	1	4	3

Directions (Q. Nos. 33-35) For each question, read the situation and choose the best sentence using the conditional.

33. I wasn't thirsty. I didn't drink the lemonade.

A. If I was thirsty, I would drink the lemonade.

B. If I had been thirsty, I would've drunk the lemonade.

C. If I would have been thirsty, I drank the lemonade.

D. If I were thirsty, I would have drunk the lemonade.

Codes

(a) Only A (b) Only B
(c) Both A and D (d) B, C and D

34. I didn't know Kavya was in town. I didn't call her.

A. If I had known Kavya was in town, I would have called her.

B. I had called Kavya if I had know she was in town.

C. I would had called Kavya if I have known she was in town.

D. I would have called Kavya, if I knew she was in town.

Codes

(a) Only B (b) Both A and C
(c) A, B and C (d) Only A

35. I didn't know watching this documentary was important for our exam. I didn't watch it.

A. If I knew this documentary was important, I had watched it.

B. If I would have known this documentary was important, I had watched it.

C. If I had known this documentary was important, I would've watched it.

D. If I knew this documentary was important, I would've watched it.

Codes

(a) Only B (b) Both A and C
(c) Both B and D (d) Only C

Chapter 05

Collocations

1 Mark Questions

Directions (Q. Nos. 1-7) Choose the best answer to fill the gap in each of the following.

1. The meeting took almost five hours so it was impossible to .... attention all the time.
(a) pay (b) give
(c) have (d) keep

2. The problem is difficult to .... under control.
(a) hold (b) do
(c) make (d) keep

3. Could you ......me a favour and post these letters on your way home?
(a) do (b) get
(c) bring (d) make

4. The news was a shock for Miguel. He stared at his friends in .... disbelief.
(a) surprised (b) overwhelmed
(c) utter (d) alarmed

5. I think we need to give this issue further .... before making a decision.
(a) communication
(b) conversation
(c) argument
(d) discussion

6. If you promise something to someone, you should .... your word.
(a) hold (b) sustain
(c) keep (d) maintain

7. It was very .... criticism, but it helped me improve.
(a) hard (b) harsh
(c) rough (d) grim

Directions (Q. Nos. 8-14) Choose the option that forms a natural-sounding collocation with the word(s).

8. Switching to a cheaper supplier was definitely a .... choice.
(a) simple (b) sane
(c) wise (d) sound

9. If you call and complain, they may .... the fee for you.
(a) waive
(b) eliminate
(c) get rid of
(d) remove

10. We have some talented young people who have a/an .... future with this company.
(a) positive
(b) bright
(c) optimistic
(d) forward looking

11. Improving education remains a .... priority for the federal government.
(a) strong
(b) great
(c) high
(d) crucial

12. The goal of the campaign is to .... awareness about pollution and overfishing in the area.
(a) produce (b) generate
(c) draw (d) raise

13. I tried to .... a glimpse of the email he was reading, but I couldn't see the screen.
(a) catch (b) capture
(c) secure (d) see

14. I have a feeling that the government has a(n) .... agenda. There is usually some ulterior motive behind these decisions.
(a) unspoken
(b) hidden
(c) unsaid
(d) concealed

Directions (Q. Nos. 15-21) Choose the correct word that collocates with the given word.

15. Sustain
(a) Minor injury (b) Cold
(c) Diarrhoea (d) Fever

16. Terrible
(a) Judgement (b) Choice
(c) Mistake (d) Apology

17. Sticky
(a) Area (b) Situation
(c) Place (d) Circumstance

18. Gut
(a) Feeling (b) Instinct
(c) Intuition (d) Conscience

19. Close
(a) Edge (b) End (c) Shave (d) Area

20. Survival
(a) Instinct (b) Feeling
(c) Ability (d) Capability

21. Cordially
(a) Ask (b) Request
(c) Presence (d) Invite

2 Marks Questions

Directions (Q. Nos. 22 and 23) Match the column A with column B to find the word that collocates the word given in column A.

22.

Column A	Column B
A. Migrant	1. Healthcare
B. Affordable	2. Equality
C. Gender	3. Justice
D. Poetic	4. Worker

Codes

	A	B	C	D		A	B	C	D
(a)	1	2	3	4	(b)	4	1	2	3
(c)	2	3	1	4	(d)	3	4	1	2

23.

Column A	Column B
A. Striking	1. Resemblance
B. Architecturally	2. Attached
C. Compromised	3. Sound
D. Emotionally	4. Security

Codes

	A	B	C	D
(a)	1	2	3	4
(b)	4	1	2	3
(c)	1	3	4	2
(d)	3	4	1	2

24. Match each noun on the left with a verb on the right.

Column A	Column B
A. an accident	1. barks
B. a dog	2. beats
C. a heart	3. shines
D. snow	4. falls
E. the sun	5. happens

Codes

	A	B	C	D	E
(a)	5	1	2	4	3
(b)	1	2	3	4	5
(c)	2	1	3	5	4
(d)	5	1	2	3	4

25. Match each verb on the left with a noun on the right. Some verbs can be followed by more than one noun but you must use each word once only.

Column A	Column B
A. do	1. breakfast
B. have	2. your breath
C. hold	3. your own business
D. mind	4. a corner
E. turn	5. a favour

Codes

	A	B	C	D	E		A	B	C	D	E
(a)	2	1	5	3	4	(b)	5	1	2	3	4
(c)	3	4	1	5	2	(d)	5	1	3	4	2

Chapter 06

Active and Passive Voice

1 Mark Questions

Directions (Q. Nos. 1-9) Change the following sentences into Passive voice.

1. We bake the biscuits over a charcoal fire.

(a) The biscuits were baked over a charcoal fire.

(b) The biscuits are being baked over a charcoal fire.

(c) The biscuits are baked over a charcoal fire.

(d) The biscuits was being baked over a charcoal fire.

2. The secretary will write the minutes of the meeting.

(a) The minutes of the meeting will be written by the secretary.

(b) The minutes of the meeting will have been written by the secretary.

(c) The minutes of the meeting are being written by the secretary.

(d) The minutes of the meeting are written by the secretary.

3. They have discussed the problem for several days.

(a) The problem is being discussed for several days.

(b) The problem is discussed for several days.

(c) The problem has been discussed for several days.

(d) The problem was discussed for several days.

4. They built that block of flats in 1973.

(a) That block of flats was built in 1973.

(b) That block of flats are built in 1973.

(c) That block of flats has been built in 1973.

(d) That block of flats were built in 1973.

5. The dog chased two squirrels.

(a) Two squirrels were chased by a dog.

(b) Two squirrels were chased by the dog.

(c) Squirrels were chased by the dog.

(d) Two squirrels are chased by the dog.

6. We can find many types of sea-shells along the sea-shore.

(a) Many types of sea-shells could be found along the sea-shore.

(b) Many types of sea-shells can be found along the sea-shore.

(c) Many types of sea-shells have been discovered along the sea-shore.

(d) Many types of sea-shells would have been discovered along the sea-shore.

7. Some one has discovered iron ore on a tiny island.

(a) Iron ore has been discovered on a tiny island by someone.
(b) Iron ore is discovered on a tiny island by someone.
(c) Iron ore are being discovered on a tiny island by someone.
(d) Iron ore had been discovered on a tiny island by someone.

8. You should peel the skins of the potatoes before you cook them.

(a) The skins of the potatoes should be peeled before they are cooked.
(b) The skins of the potatoes could be peeled before they are cooked.
(c) The skins of the potatoes should have been peeled before they are cooked.
(d) The skins of the potatoes could be peeled before cooking.

9. People have referred to the jellyfish, the star fish, the cuttlefish and the crayfish as 'fish' though they are not.

(a) The jellyfish, the star fish, the cuttlefish and the crayfish are being referred to as fish though they are not.
(b) The jellyfish, the starfish, the cuttlefish and crayfish have been referred to as fish though they are not.
(c) The jellyfish, the starfish, the cuttle-fish and the crayfish will be referred to as 'fish' though they are not.
(d) The jellyfish, the starfish, the cuttlefish and crayfish had been said to be as fish though they are not.

Directions (Q. Nos. 10-15) Given below are sentences in active and passive voice. Fill in the blanks of active/passive of these sentences.

10. They have seen the movie on Monday.
The movie .... on Monday.

(a) have been seen by they
(b) have been seen by them
(c) has been seen by they
(d) has been seen by them

11. A letter is being written to the President of India by Rahul.
Rahul .... a letter to the President of India.

(a) is writing (b) has written
(c) writes (d) had written

12. By then, the children will have completely constructed the projects for the exhibition.
By then, the projects for the exhibition .... by the children.

(a) will had been completely construct
(b) will have been completely constructed
(c) will has been completely construct
(d) will be completed constructed

13. The control room is notifying police that three prisoners have escaped.
Police .... by the control room that there prisoners have escaped.

(a) is being notified
(b) are being notified
(c) have been notified
(d) are notified

14. The experiment has been conducted by the scientists to test the hypothesis.
Scientists .... the experiment to test the hypothesis.

(a) have conduct
(b) have been conducting
(c) have conducted
(d) had been conducting

15. What did the Mad Hatter say in 'Alice in Wonderland'?
What .... the Mad Hatter in 'Alice in Wonderland'?

(a) was said by (b) is says by
(c) is say by (d) was said from

Directions (Q. Nos. 16-25) Here is a news report about a storm. Choose the correct verb from the options given below to complete the report.

Millions of crores worth of damage ....**(16)**.... by the cyclone which ....**(17)**.... across the North of Odisha coast last night. The river Teesa ....**(18)**.... its bank after heavy rains. Many people ....**(19)**.... from the floods by firefighters who ....**(20)**.... hundreds of call for help. Wind speeds ....**(21)**.... ninety miles an hour in some places, Roads ....**(22)**.... by fallen trees and electricity lines ....**(23)**.... down, leaving thousands of homes without electricity. Everything possible ....**(24)**.... to get things back to normal, a spokesman ....**(25)**....

Options

16. (a) has caused (b) has been caused (c) was caused (d) is caused

17. (a) was swamped (b) had swamped (c) swamped (d) have swamped

18. (a) swept (b) has swept (c) did sweep (d) had swept

19. (a) rescued (b) was rescued (c) have been rescued (d) were rescued

20. (a) received (b) had received (c) has received (d) is receiving

21. (a) reached (b) have reached (c) had reached (d) reaches

22. (a) blocked (b) were blocked (c) has blocked (d) have been blocked

23. (a) were cut (b) cut (c) have been cut (d) was cut

24. (a) is doing (b) is being done (c) done (d) has been done

25. (a) said (b) has said (c) has been said (d) will be said

Directions (Q. Nos. 26-34) Complete the text with the correct passive forms.

Aditya had a job interview last week at a small company based in Noida, not too far from his home. The company had advertised for an office assistant. The application ....**(26)**.... on line. About two weeks later Aditya ....**(27)**.... for an interview at the company's head office. He ....**(28)**.... by the office manager and asked to sit in the conference room. The interview ....**(29)**.... by a panel of three directors. After the interview was over Aditya ....**(30)**.... a chance to ask any questions of his term. Then he ....**(31)**.... to a short tour of the office. He ....**(32)**.... that he ....**(33)**.... within a week. Yesterday Aditya ....**(34)**.... a position in the company.

Options

26. (a) were submitted (b) had been submitted (c) was submitted (d) had submitted

27. (a) had been called (b) was called (c) was being called (d) had called

28. (a) greeted (b) had been greeted (c) was greeted (d) would be greeted

29. (a) was conducted (b) was being conducted (c) had been conducted (d) would be conducted

30. (a) would be given (b) had been given
(c) was being given (d) was given

31. (a) had been taken (b) would be taken
(c) was taken (d) were taken

32. (a) told (b) was being told
(c) had been told (d) was told

33. (a) would be contacted
(b) had contacted
(c) was contacted
(d) will be contacted

34. (a) had been offered
(b) would be offered
(c) was offered
(d) was being offered

Directions (Q. Nos. 35-40) Complete the sentence in passive voice by choosing the correct option.

35. A lot of property ....by the fire.
(a) have been destroyed
(b) destroyed
(c) has been destroyed
(d) will be destroyed

36. The animals .... when we visited the Zoo yesterday.
(a) was being fed (b) is fed
(c) are being fed (d) were being fed

37. The vegetables.......... before they are cooked.
(a) is washed (b) be washed
(c) are washed (d) was washed

38. This road .... by the town council.
(a) is being repaired (b) repaired
(c) is repairing (d) repairs

39. He..........guilty of murder.
(a) found (b) was found
(c) has been found (d) is found

40. The boy ....by the noise.
(a) is frightening
(b) was frightened
(c) frightened
(d) have been frightened

2 Marks Questions

Directions (Q. Nos. 41 and 42) Replace the underlined words with correct form of Passive voice.

41. A new bill was introducted **(i)** in the Parliament during the next session. The draft of the bill examiners **(ii)** currently by experts. It will be sent **(iii)** to the experts in December last year.

(i) (a) is introduced
(b) will be introduced
(c) is being introduced
(d) has been introduced

(ii) (a) is being examined
(b) was being examined
(c) will be examined
(d) are being examined

(iii) (a) was being sent
(b) is being sent
(c) had been sent
(d) was sent

42. Vibha is feeling proud of her father because he is elected **(i)** as an M.P. But he is being disliked **(ii)** by the people for his wrong practices.

(i) (a) will be elected
(b) has been elected
(c) elects
(d) had been elected

(ii) (a) is disliked
(b) was being disliked
(c) dislikes
(d) disliking

Directions (Q. Nos. 43 and 44) Choose the correct passive form from the options given below.

43. 1. Some trees have been planted by the gardener.
2. Some advice was been given to you by the Doctor.
3. The hotel has redecorated by a famous designer.

Which of the above statement is correct?

(a) Only 1 (b) Only 2
(c) 1 and 3 (d) 1 and 2

44. 1. The product will be advertised on the television.
2. My assignment has been finished.
3. The fence is being repaired by some one?

Which of the above statements is correct?

(a) 1 and 2 (b) 2 and 3
(c) 1 and 3 (d) 1, 2 and 3

45. Identify which of the following sentences is written in Passive voice?

A. Over half of the graduating class went to college in the fall.
B. The committee is considering a public transportation proposal.
C. The state exam was passed by over half of the students who took it.
D. The researchers will publish their findings in a report.

Codes

(a) Only A (b) Both A and B
(c) Only C (d) Both B and D

46. Identify which of the following sentences are in Passive voice?

A. Two boys were seen near the gym yesterday.
B. The telephone has rung ten times already.
C. Bela's bracelet has silver charms.
D. Lata's red sweater was lying on the couch.

Codes

(a) A (b) B (c) C (d) D

47. Match the column and choose the correct option.

Column A	Column B	Column C
(i) The watch	A. must be read	1. by the students
(ii) The answers	B. was given	2. by every one
(iii) This book	C. have been learnt	3. to me by my grandfather

Which is the correct pairing?

(a) (i)-A-1, (ii)-B-2, (iii)-C-3
(b) (i)-B-3, (ii)-C-1, (iii)-A-2
(c) (i)-C-2, (ii)-A-3, (iii)-B-1
(d) (i)-B-2, (ii)-C-3, (iii)-A-1

48. Choose the correct passive form of the given sentence from the options given below.

Robert Browning, wrote the poem 'The Pied Piper of Hamelin, for the son of his good friend William Macready.

(a) The poem 'The Pied Piper of Hamelin is written by Robert Browning for the son of good friend William Macready.
(b) The poem 'The Pied Piper of Hamelin' was written by Robert Browning for the son of his good friend William Macready.
(c) The poem 'The Pied Piper of Hamelin' is being written by Robert Browning for the son of his good friend William Macready.
(d) The poem 'The Pied Piper of Hamelin' has been written by Robert Browning for the son of his good friend William Macready.

Chapter 07

Direct and Indirect Speech

1 Mark Questions

Directions (Q. Nos. 1-6) Change the following sentences into indirect speech by choosing the correct option.

1. He says, "Switzerland is the heaven on Earth".

(a) He said that Switzerland is thc heaven on Earth.

(b) He told that Switzerland was the heaven on Earth.

(c) He says that Switzerland is the heaven on Earth.

(d) He tells that Switzerland is the heaven on Earth.

2. The shopkeeper says, "Prices are shooting up alarmingly."

(a) The shopkeeper says that prices are shooting up alarmingly.

(b) The shopkeeper said that prices are shooting up alarmingly.

(c) The shopkeeper says that prices were shooting up alarmingly.

(d) The shopkeeper tells that prices will be shooting up alarmingly.

3. She said, "Nobody can solve the problem."

(a) She said that nobody can solve that problem.

(b) She said that nobody could solve the problem.

(c) She told that nobody can solve the problem.

(d) She said nobody could have solved the problem.

4. Sheela said to Meera, "I shall be taking a test".

(a) Sheela said to Meera that she shall be taking a test.

(b) Sheela told Meera that she would be taking a test.

(c) Sheela said to Meera that she will take a test.

(d) Sheela said to Meera that she should be taking a test.

5. Antony said, "Martin has gone home".

(a) Antony told that Martin has gone home.

(b) Antony said that Martin has gone home.

(c) Antony said that Martin had gone home.

(d) Antony said that Martin would have gone home.

6. She said to me, "How have you done this sum?"

(a) She asked me how have I done this sum?

(b) She asked me how I had done that sum.

(c) She asked me how did I do that sum.

(d) She asked me how I did that sum.

Directions (Q. Nos. 7-13) Read the conversation and then Report what Chitra said to Naveen and Naveen said to Chitra and fill in the blanks with the help of options given below.

Naveen	How long have you been in Australia?
Chitra	Eight weeks.
Naveen	Are you enjoying your stay here?
Chitra	Yes, I am enjoying it a lot.
Naveen	Have you been here before?
Chitra	Yes, I've been to Australia many times.
Naveen	What are you doing here?
Chitra	I've come to meet my relatives who have settled here.
Naveen	Are you staying with them or in a hotel?
Chitra	No, I'm staying with some friends.
Naveen	Where do they stay?
Chitra	They have a flat in the heart of the city.
Naveen	How long will you stay here?
Chitra	I'm leaving in March 2015.

7. Chitra said that she .... in Australia for eight weeks.
(a) has been (b) had been
(c) have been (d) is

8. Chitra said that she .... her stay a lot.
(a) has been enjoying
(b) had been enjoying
(c) was enjoying
(d) have been enjoying

9. Chitra said that she .... to Australia many times.
(a) has been (b) was
(c) had been (d) were

10. Chitra said that she .... with some friends.
(a) has been staying (b) is staying
(c) was staying (d) will be staying

11. She said that her .... a flat in the heart of the city.
(a) friends have (b) friends do have
(c) friends had (d) friends are having

12. She said she .... in March 2015.
(a) will be leaving (b) was leaving
(c) is leaving (d) would be leaving

13. She said that she .... to meet her relatives in Australia.
(a) have come (b) has come
(c) had come (d) came

Directions (Q. Nos. 14-19) Choose the correct option to complete the sentences given below.

14. I asked her ....
(a) what is the answer
(b) what the answer was
(c) what was the answer
(d) what would be the answer

15. Do you remember ....
(a) when is her birthday
(b) when her birthday is
(c) when will be her birthday
(d) when would be her birthday

16. I requested them ....
(a) not going there
(b) do not go there
(c) not to go there
(d) should not go there

17. He said ....
(a) he will study for the exam
(b) he had study for the exam
(c) he would study for the exam
(d) he may study for the exam

18. The personal officer will show you ....

(a) which cubicle you had been allocated.
(b) which cubicle you have been allocated.
(c) which cubicle you will be allocated.
(d) which cubicle you would be allocated.

19. We can't imagine how ....

(a) the old man did cope up all these years.
(b) the old man coped up all these years.
(c) the old man has coped up all these years.
(d) the old man would have coped up all these years.

Directions (Q. Nos. 20-27) Here, it is a report of a telephone message on a tape recorder by a secretary. Write out the actual words that you think Mr Natarajan used.

Mr Natarajan said that he was very sorry that he could not attend the sales conference on Monday. He was leaving for Shimla that evening and would not be back till Wednesday. He wondered if Mr Salim could go to the sales conference instead. He would appreciate it if he could know by that evening, so that he could ask Mr Salim to make his travel arrangements. He apologised for any inconvenience caused.

"I am very sorry ......**(20)**...... to attend the sales conference on Monday. ......**(21)**...... for Shimla this evening and ......**(22)**...... till Wednesday. I was ......**(23)**...... if Salim ......**(24)**...... to sales conference instead. ......**(25)**...... let me know by this evening? ......**(26)**...... ask Salim to make his travel arrangements.
......**(27)**...... once again for the inconvenience caused."

Choose the best option to complete Mr Natarajan's words.

20. (a) I don't think I'll be able to
(b) I won't think I shall be able to
(c) I don't think of I would be able to
(d) I didn't think I would be able

21. (a) I will be leaving (b) I was leaving
(c) I am leaving (d) I shall be leaving

22. (a) I'll not be back
(b) I am not coming back
(c) I would not be back
(d) I was not coming back

23. (a) thinking (b) wondering
(c) assuming (d) not sure

24. (a) Would go (b) Could go
(c) Would be going (d) Will go

25. (a) Will you please (b) Could you please
(c) Would you please (d) Shall you please

26. (a) I will then (b) I could then
(c) I shall then (d) I would then

27. (a) I am sorry (b) I will be sorry
(c) I was sorry (d) I would be sorry

Directions (Q. Nos. 28-32) Choose the correct option to complete the indirect speech.

28. Mary "I went skiing."
Jill : Mary said that she ...... skiing.
(a) went (b) had gone
(c) have gone (d) has gone

29. Manisha "I have never been to London."
Neelam : Manisha said that she ...... never been to London.
(a) had (b) has (c) have (d) will have

30. Mary "I will go downtown tomorrow."
Neelam : Mary said that she ...... go downtown ....
(a) an/on Friday
(b) will/the next day
(c) would/the next day
(d) would have/ the next day.

31. Manisha "I am going to play Tennis today."
Neelam : Manisha said that she .... to play Tennis ....
(a) is going/this day
(b) was going/that day
(c) will be going/tomorrow
(d) has been going/today

32. Madhu "I went to bed early last night."
Jeevan : Madhu said that she ...... to bed early ....
(a) has gone/yesterday
(b) had gone/the night before
(c) had gone/last night
(d) has gone/the previous night

Directions (Q. Nos. 33-35) Replace the underlined words with suitable word.

Anne told a confectioner that she <u>wants</u> **(33)** to order a big birthday cake. The confectioner asked when her birthday <u>is</u> **(34)** Anne replied it was the following day. The confectioner told her to <u>collected</u> **(35)** it by noon.

Choose the correct option.

33. (a) wanting (b) wanted
(c) want (d) wants

34. (a) will (b) was
(c) were (d) would be

35. (a) be collect (b) collecting
(c) collect (d) collects

2 Marks Questions

36. Choose the correct option.
1. I asked to him where he lived.
2. They told me that they would wait for me.
3. My mother asked me not to jump on her bed.

Which of the above statements are correct?
(a) 1 and 2
(b) 2 and 3
(c) 1 and 3
(d) All of the above

37. Choose the correct option.
1. He said that two and two make four.
2. She asked me if Raju was my friend.
3. Maneesh said that he may go to Delhi the next day.

Which of the above statements is/are correct?
(a) Only 1 (b) Only 2
(c) All of these (d) None of these

38. Match the column and choose the correct option.

Column A	Column B	Column C
(i) I told him	A. that they were	1. go for a walk
(ii) He proposed to me	B. that he must not	2. leaving that night
(iii) They said	C. that we should	3. tell lies

Choose the correct option
(a) (i)-A-1, (ii)-B-2, (iii)-B-3
(b) (i)-B-3, (ii)-C-1, (iii)-A-2
(c) (i)-C-1, (ii)-B-3, (iii)-A-2
(d) (i)-B-3, (ii)-C-2, (iii)-A-1

39. Match the column .

Column A	Column B	Column C
(i) He told	A. that honesty	1. he had done his best
(ii) The principal announced	B. that the next day	2. is the best policy
(iii) The teacher said	C. his parents that	3. would be a holiday

Choose the correct option

(a) (i)-C-1, (ii)-B-3, (iii)-A-2
(b) (i)-B-2, (ii)-C-3, (iii)-A-1
(c) (i)-A-3, (ii)-B-2, (iii)-C-1
(d) (i)-C-3, (ii)-A-1, (iii)-B-2

40. Choose the correct option.

(i) **Assertion** (A) 'He said he had been playing' will change to 'He said that he had been playing' in indirect narration.

(ii) **Reason** (R) If the reporting verb is in past perfect continuous tense, it does not change in indirect narration.

Which is correct?

(a) Both A and R are true and R is the correct explanation of A
(b) Both A and R are true, but R is not the correct explanation of A
(c) A is true, but R is false
(d) A is false, but R is true

41. Choose the correct option.

(i) **Assertion** (A) He tells "Ram is playing" is incorrect statement.

(ii) **Reason** (R) If the reporting verb is in present, the tense does not change.

Which is correct?

(a) Both A and R are correct and R is the explanation of A
(b) Both A and R are correct, but R is not the explanation of A
(c) A is true, but R is false
(d) A is false, but R is true

Chapter 08

Jumbled Words/Sentences

1 Mark Questions

Directions (Q. Nos. 1-10) Rearrange the following parts to form a meaningful sentence.

1. **P** for thousands of years
Q famous symbols of ancient civilisations
R monuments have been created
S as they are often the most durable and
(a) SRQP (b) QPRS (c) PRSQ (d) RPSQ

2. **P** is one of the most widely used indicators
Q of ecosystems and their biodiversity
R for assessing the condition
S the conservation status of plants and animals
(a) SPRQ (b) SRQP (c) QRPS (d) PQRS

3. **P** for a short time where a new, innovative, or much-improved product
Q the practice of 'price skimming'
R is launched into a market
S involves charging a relatively high price
(a) QSPR (b) RSQP (c) PRSQ (d) RQSP

4. **P** by an emperor named Shah Jahan
Q the Taj Mahal is a
R in memory of his wife Mumtaz Mahal
S beautiful monument built in 1631
(a) QPRS (b) QSRP (c) PQRS (d) QSPR

5. **P** was designed by the British architect George Wittet and
Q the Gateway of India
R in the year 1924
S was opened for general public
(a) QSPR (b) QPSR (c) PQSR (d) SRQP

6. **P** in the benefits of expanding markets for
Q the new agriculture of high-value activities
R commercial smallholders deliver
S surpluses to food markets and share
(a) RSPQ (b) QSRP (c) PSQR (d) RQSP

7. **P** is viable or successful
Q that a company
R the purpose of advertising is
S to reassure employees or shareholders
(a) RQSP (b) RPSQ (c) QPRS (d) RSQP

8. **P** is regarded as an enduring symbol
Q one of the world's greatest cultural monuments
R of ancient Greece and of Athenian democracy and
S the Parthenon
(a) SPRQ (b) RPSQ
(c) QPRS (d) PRQS

9. **P** through their work capacity and help
Q the employee management tools track
R to differentiate between the skilled, semi-skilled and the unskilled people
S the efficiency of the employees
(a) RPSQ (b) SPRQ
(c) RQSP (d) QSPR

10. **P** about 40% of Indians had first-hand experience
Q transparency International reports
R of paying bribes or using a contact
S to get a job done in public office
(a) SPRQ (b) SPQR (c) QPRS (d) RQSP

Directions (Q. Nos. 11-18) Rearrange the words to make a meaningful sentence.

11. I/have/risk/taken/saving/her/a/in/great
(a) I taken have a great risk in saving her.
(b) A great risk have I taken in saving her.
(c) Her have taken I a great risk in saving.
(d) I have taken a great risk in saving her.

12. the road/of/obey/we/rules/the/must
(a) The rules of the road we must obey.
(b) We obey the must rules of the road.
(c) Wc must obey the rules of the road.
(d) We must obey the road of the rules.

13. storm/clouds/the/seen/were/dark/before
(a) Storm were seen before the dark clouds.
(b) Dark clouds were seen before the storm.
(c) Dark clouds were seen the before storm.
(d) The storm before the dark clouds were seen.

14. in studies/he is/in games/and/good/both
(a) He is both good in studies and in games.
(b) He is both good in and studies games.
(c) He is good in both studies and games.
(d) He is good both in studies and in games.

15. the teachers/a/is/favourite/of all/Ramesh
(a) Ramesh is a favourite of all the teachers.
(b) Ramesh the teachers is favourite of all.
(c) All the teachers is favourite of Ramesh.
(d) Ramesh is the favourite of a all teachers.

16. from God/a precious/life/is/to/gift/us
(a) Life is a precious gift to us from God.
(b) To us, life is a precious gift from God.
(c) From God, life is a precious gift to us.
(d) Life is a precious gift from us to God.

17. park/my house/is/there/a/near
(a) There is a house near my park.
(b) There is a park near my house.
(c) Near my house is there a park.
(d) My house is a there near the park.

18. playing/they/in/are/ground/the/cricket
(a) The cricket are playing they in the ground.
(b) They are playing cricket in the ground.
(c) They are in the ground playing cricket.
(d) They are playing in the ground cricket.

2 Marks Questions

Directions (Q. Nos. 19-22) Multiple sentences are written in a random way. You have to rearrange the jumbled sentences into a meaningful paragraph.

19. (i) It has been so from time immemorial.
(ii) It is necessary to have a library.
(iii) Library is a centre of learning.
(iv) The selected books should enchant us.
(v) our teachers had their libraries.

(a) (iv), (ii), (v), (i), (iii)
(b) (iii), (i), (v), (ii), (iv)
(c) (i), (ii), (iii), (iv), (v)
(d) (iii), (ii), (i), (iv), (v)

20. (i) If they are dissatisfied, they have a cause to complain.
(ii) Rather they are an embodiment of patience.
(iii) Teachers ought to set an example.

(iv) Yet they should exercise restraint.
(v) Patience is one of the greatest virtues.
(a) (iii), (ii), (i), (iv), (v)
(b) (v), (iv), (iii), (ii), (i)
(c) (i), (ii), (iii), (iv), (v)
(d) (iii), (i), (iv), (ii), (v)

21. (i) It dislodged the green spectacles from Denton's nose, and for a moment his eyes were exposed.
(ii) To Oliver it was fun, but Denton evidently did not relish it.
(iii) He replaced them hurriedly, but not in time. Oliver's sharp eyes detected him.
(iv) The road was a bad one, jolting the vehicle without mercy.
(v) At last one jolt came, nearly overturning the conveyance.
(a) (iv), (ii), (v), (iii), (i)
(b) (iii), (iv), (v), (ii), (i)
(c) (iv), (ii), (v), (i), (iii)
(d) (v), (iv), (ii), (i), (iii)

22. (i) With the passage of time, vices become more apparent and virtues become objects of jealousy and envy, thereby causing contempt and hatred in the hearts of each other.
(ii) They become familiar with not only strengths but also weaknesses of each other's characters.
(iii) Generally people think that familiarity should breed love, mutual understanding and tolerance.
(iv) They expect that coming together of two persons should bring them closer and forge the bond of kinship between them.
(v) But when two persons come closer, they come to know not only strengths but also weaknesses of each other's character.
(a) (ii), (iv), (i), (iii), (v)
(b) (iii), (iv), (v), (ii), (i)
(c) (iii), (ii), (i), (v), (iv)
(d) (ii), (iii), (iv), (i), (v)

Directions (Q. Nos. 23 and 24) Rearrange the following sentences to make meaningful paragraphs.

23. (i) To much of the labour movement, it symbolises the brutality of the upper classes.
(ii) And to everybody watching, the current mess over foxhunting, symbolises the government's weakness.
(iii) To foxhunting supporters, Labour's 1991 manifesto commitment to ban it symbolises the party's metropolitan roots and hostility to the countryside.
(iv) Small issues sometimes have large symbolic power.
(v) To those who enjoy thundering across the country-side in red coats after foxes, foxhunting symbolises the ancient roots of rural lives.
(a) (iv), (v), (i), (iii), (ii)
(b) (v), (iii), (iv), (ii), (i)
(c) (iii), (v), (i); (ii), (iv)
(d) (iv), (ii), (i), (v), (iii)

24. (i) Hitler said he was in a rush and asked Ribbentrop if he could be taken next, but Ribentrop insisted it would look bad for the Foreign Office if he were passed over.
(ii) Hitler thereupon made a quick phone call and Ribbentrop was immediately transferred to the Afrika Korps.
(iii) In the spring of 1940, a large Mercedes pulled up in front of my barbershop at 127 Koenigstrasse, Hitler walked in and said, "I just want a light trim – and don't take too much off the top."
(iv) I explained to him there would be a brief wait because von Ribbentrop was ahead of him.
(a) (iii), (i), (iv), (ii)
(b) (iii), (iv), (i), (ii)
(c) (iii), (ii), (iv), (i)
(d) (iii), (i), (ii), (iv)

Chapter 09

Synonyms and Antonyms

1 Mark Questions

Directions (Q. Nos. 1-10) In the following questions, out of the four alternatives, choose the one which best expresses the meaning of the given word.

1. Garnish
(a) Honour (b) Respect
(c) Obey (d) Adorn

2. Abandon
(a) Excuse (b) Forsake
(c) Urge (d) Risk

3. Odious
(a) Hateful (b) Rotten
(c) Infamous (d) Sick

4. Petition
(a) Rotation
(b) Administration
(c) Appeal
(d) Vocation

5. Proposition
(a) Intimation (b) Protestation
(c) Proposal (d) Invitation

6. Vivacious
(a) Imaginary (b) Spirited
(c) Perceptible (d) Languid

7. Sporadic
(a) Timely (b) Scattered
(c) Frequent (d) Irrelevant

8. Persevere
(a) Fickle (b) Persist
(c) Constant (d) Polite

9. Heralded
(a) Suspected (b) Publicised
(c) Dragged (d) Objective

10. Multitude
(a) Impoverished (b) Solitude
(c) Acknowledged (d) Plenty

Directions (Q. Nos. 11-20) In each of the following question, choose the one which is most nearly the same in meaning to the word underlined in bold in the sentence.

11. His judicious handling of the matter saved the situation from going out of control.
(a) Nervous (b) Helpful
(c) Sensible (d) Cautious

12. Ritu asked Rashmi not to meddle in her affairs.
(a) Intercede (b) Impose
(c) Cross (d) Interfere

13. The story is too fantastic to be credible.
(a) Praiseworthy
(b) Readable
(c) Believable
(d) False

14. Catching snakes can be hazardous for people untrained in the art.
(a) Dangerous (b) Difficult
(c) Harmful (d) Tricky

15. A civilised Roman banquet was a thing of great richness, style and decorum.
(a) Palace (b) Feast
(c) Ornament (d) Table

16. We must eradicate corruption.
(a) Minimise (b) Control
(c) Condemn (d) Uproot

17. The weavers have to do monotonous work.
(a) Repetitive (b) Exhausting
(c) Irksome (d) Autonomous

18. He gave such a vivid description of the house we wanted to rent that we didn't have to look at it.
(a) Simple (b) Detailed
(c) Clear (d) Confuse

19. There is not a single word that is redundant in the report.
(a) Bombastic (b) Unimportant
(c) Flowery (d) None of these

20. The guests were offended by his uncouth manners.
(a) Wasteful (b) Dirty
(c) Undesirable (d) Ungracious

Directions (Q. Nos. 21-26) Read the paragraph below. Rewrite it by replacing each underlined word with a synonym from the list.

I was struggling to **(21)** complete my Maths homework. I had gone to my big brother for help, but he hadn't **(22)** contributed very much. I had a very hard time when I had to **(23)** calculate the answers for problems like these, and i wanted very much to **(24)** conclude working on this assignment. But it seemed like the harder I worked, the more **(25)** confused I became. I just don't know if I'm **(26)** capable of learning how to divide fractions.

21. (a) finish (b) incomplete
(c) final (d) end

22. (a) done (b) finished
(c) helped (d) given

23. (a) understand (b) sum
(c) operations (d) reckon

24. (a) wind up (b) finish
(c) proper (d) quality

25. (a) polite (b) puzzled
(c) anxious (d) troubled

26. (a) qualified (b) ruthless
(c) energetic (d) anxious

Directions (Q. Nos. 27-36) In the following questions, choose the word opposite in meaning to the given word.

27. Exorbitant
(a) Barbaric (b) Famished
(c) Counterfeit (d) Moderate

28. Humane
(a) Cruel (b) Proud
(c) Cheerful (d) Tranquil

29. Obsolete
(a) Heated (b) Desolate
(c) Contemporary (d) Automatic

30. Suppress
(a) Stimulate (b) Encourage
(c) Abandon (d) Smother

31. Terminate
(a) Hasten
(b) Depart
(c) Begin
(d) Change

32. Thrive
(a) Succeed (b) Deteriorate
(c) Worry (d) Tremble

33. Mundane
(a) Extraordinary (b) Regular
(c) Severe (d) Visionary

34. Consensus
(a) Acceptance (b) Opinion
(c) Disagreement (d) Permission

35. Genuine
(a) General (b) Real
(c) Fake (d) Genie

36. Flexible
(a) Rigid (b) Cruel
(c) Humble (d) Easy

Directions (Q. Nos. 37-46) Choose the word which is most opposite in meaning of the word underlined as used in the sentences.

37. Professors are generally serious about what they say.
(a) Jolly (b) Thoughtful
(c) Smug (d) Insincere

38. His knowledge of the subject is quite extensive.
(a) Ordinary (b) Little
(c) Limited (d) Simple

39. My uncle is very wealthy, but rather parsimonious in his habits.
(a) Extravagant (b) Stingy
(c) Careless (d) Strict

40. The government is taking measures to augment the country's food supply.
(a) Prohibit (b) Decrease
(c) Surpass (d) Compensate

41. Of all the companions of our joyous ascent, there were only the two of us left.
(a) Decent (b) Descent
(c) Distant (d) Descendant

42. Sherlock Holmes is a fictitious character.
(a) Real (b) Imaginative
(c) Fancy (d) Foreign

43. The revised pay scale is uniform.
(a) Equal (b) Similar
(c) Opposite (d) Varied

44. She is slender in figure.
(a) Strong (b) Well-built
(c) Stout (d) Slim

45. The minister was accused of indulging in nepotism.
(a) Impartiality (b) Hatred
(c) Condemnation (d) Indifference

46. He could not confirm that he had made any such statement.
(a) Reject (b) Avoid (c) Deny (d) Refuse

2 Marks Questions

Directions (Q. Nos. 47 and 48) In each of the following questions four words are given out of which two words are nearly the same in meaning. Find the correct combination.

47. (i) Enthralling (ii) Respecting
(iii) Projecting (iv) Alluring
(a) (i)-(ii) (b) (ii)-(iii)
(c) (iii)-(iv) (d) (i)-(iv)

48. (i) Conversion (ii) Resistance
(iii) Substitution (iv) Cessation
(a) (i)-(ii) (b) (iii)-(iv)
(c) (i)-(iv) (d) (ii)-(iv)

49. Match the words given in column A with their synonyms given in column B.

Column A	Column B
A. improvise	1. dubious, far-fetched
B. impound	2. ambiguous, approximate
C. improbable	3. invent and perform
D. imprecise	4. seize legally
	5. not original, copying

Codes

	A	B	C	D
(a)	5	4	3	2
(b)	3	4	1	2
(c)	3	2	4	5
(d)	1	2	3	4

50. Match the words given in column A with their synonyms given in column B.

Column A	Column B
A. Grim	1. Brilliance
B. Splendour	2. Shine
C. Gleam	3. A view
D. Vista	4. Stern

Codes

	A	B	C	D
(a)	2	4	3	1
(b)	1	4	3	2
(c)	3	2	1	4
(d)	4	1	2	3

Directions (Q. Nos. 51 and 52) Find the antonyms of the underlined word from the options given below.

51. Some people mess up their houses with <u>ever lasting</u> rubbish.

(i) Lasting (ii) Temporary
(iii) Changing (iv) Endless
(v) Eternal

(a) (iii), (iv) and (v)
(b) (i), (ii) and (iv)
(c) (ii), (iii) and (v)
(d) (i), (ii) and (iii)

52. Raju had <u>apparently</u> changed his mind.

(i) Obscure (ii) Lucid
(iii) Confused (iv) Perplexed
(v) Irrational

(a) (ii), (iii), (iv) and (i)
(b) (iii), (iv) and (v)
(c) (i), (ii), (iii) and (v)
(d) (i), (iii), (iv) and (v)

Chapter 10

One Word Substitution

1 Mark Questions

Directions (Q. Nos. 1-10) Choose one word for the given sentences.

1. The Study of Ancient Societies
(a) History (b) Archaeology
(c) Anthropology (d) Etymology

2. A practice of having more than one husband
(a) Polygyny (b) Polyandry
(c) Polygamy (d) Polytrophy

3. The Government wing responsible for making rules
(a) Judiciary (b) Legislature
(c) Executive (d) Court

4. A person who sacrifices his life for a cause
(a) Soldier (b) Revolutionary
(c) Martyr (d) Patriot

5. A person who renounces the world and practices self discipline in order to attain salvation.
(a) Sceptic (b) Ascetic
(c) Devotee (d) Antiquarian

6. One who abandons his religious faith.
(a) Apostate (b) Prostate
(c) Profane (d) Agnostic

7. Story of old time gods or heroes.
(a) Lyric (b) Epic
(c) Legend (d) Romance

8. One who believes in the power of fate.
(a) Fatalist (b) Optimist
(c) Pessimist (d) Parsimonious

9. A person who regards the whole world as his country.
(a) Cosmopolitan (b) Fratricide
(c) Altruist (d) Aristocrat

10. A person who is indifferent to pains and pleasures of life.
(a) Stoic (b) Sadist
(c) Psychiatrist (d) Aristocrat

Directions (Q. Nos. 11-18) Choose one word for the underlined phrases.

11. She <u>makes it certain</u> that she will never fight with her best friend over a petty thing like this.
(a) Assures (b) Insures
(c) Ensures (d) Seizures

12. This is his first press conference with the media, he is anxious because <u>he speaks less</u>.
(a) Sullen (b) Terse
(c) Garrulous (d) Reticent

13. My brother is a theatre artist who performs and <u>expresses stories or thoughts through gestures</u>.
(a) Pantomime (b) Mimic
(c) Depictions (d) Ham

14. Every Wednesday at the Ganesha temple my father gives alms to poor people, he loves to help the needy and put others first.

(a) Altruist (b) Swindler
(c) Misanthropic (d) Antagonist

15. They organised a house party for Sara's birthday but she does not get excited easily even if you put in a lot of effort and emotion.

(a) Gregarious (b) Placid
(c) Inclement (d) Frenzied

16. We have bought a new machine for our mother to help her in household chores, the machine can easily be carried anywhere.

(a) Cartable (b) Portable
(c) Potable (d) Relatable

17. My aunt cannot stay in the hospital for 5 minutes because she has a fear of confined places.

(a) Agoraphobia (b) Enochlophobia
(c) Claustrophobia (d) Stasiphobia

18. Jackson is a highly skilled musician; he is an expert guitarist in his college band, he will go a long way in this profession.

(a) Amateur
(b) Virtuoso
(c) Dabbler
(d) Neophyte

2 Marks Questions

Directions (Q. Nos. 19-21) In the following exercise, column A has phrases and column B has one word that can be substituted for the phrase. Match the phrases in column A with their one word substitution in column (B).

19.

Column A	Column B
A. One who is all powerful	1. Fatal
B. One who fluently speaks many languages	2. Solicitor
C. A legal advisor	3. Omnipotent
D. A disease that causes death	4. Polyglot

Codes

	A	B	C	D		A	B	C	D
(a)	3	4	2	1	(b)	1	2	3	4
(c)	3	1	2	4	(d)	2	4	1	3

20.

Column A	Column B
A. That cannot be defeated	1. Misanthrope
B. Hater of mankind	2. Opaque
C. Not allowing the passage of light	3. Invincible
D. An assembly of worshippers	4. Congregation

Codes

	A	B	C	D		A	B	C	D
(a)	3	1	2	4	(b)	2	4	1	3
(c)	1	2	3	4	(d)	4	3	2	1

21.

	Column A	Column B
A.	A short summary of a book or speech	1. Confiscate
B.	Science dealing with heredity	2. Monarchy
C.	Government by king/ queen	3. Synopsis
D.	To seize by authority	4. Genetics

Codes

	A	B	C	D		A	B	C	D
(a)	3	4	2	1	(b)	2	4	3	1
(c)	1	2	3	4	(d)	4	3	2	1

22. Choose the correct pair of one word substitution.

1. Fastidious – one who cannot be pleased
2. Prejudiced – to be biased against
3. Epitaph – words or phrases inscribed on a tomb
4. Instigation – the act of provoking and goading a man

(a) 1, 2 and 3
(b) 2, 3 and 4
(c) 1, 3 and 4
(d) All of these

23. Choose the incorrect one word substitution.

1. Excursion – scarcity of food
2. Elocution – style of speaking well
3. Famine – a short journey made by a group of people
4. Protagonist – the chief character in a story or drama

(a) 1 and 2 (b) 1 and 3
(c) 2 and 4 (d) 2 and 3

Chapter 11

Idioms and Phrases

1 Mark Questions

Directions (Q. Nos. 1-10) Given below are some idioms together with their meanings given in the options. Choose the appropriate option.

1. To make a clean breast of
(a) To gain prominence
(b) To praise oneself
(c) To confess without reserve
(d) To destroy before it blooms

2. To Keep one's temper
(a) To become hungry
(b) To be in good mood
(c) To preserve one's energy
(d) To be aloof from

3. To end in smoke
(a) To make completely understand
(b) To ruin oneself
(c) To excite great applause
(d) To overcome someone

4. To be above board
(a) To have a good height
(b) To be honest in any business deal
(c) To have no debts
(d) To try to be beautiful

5. To put one's hand to plough
(a) To take up agricultural farming
(b) To take a difficult task
(c) To get entangled into unnecessary things
(d) Take interest in technical work

6. To leave someone in lurch
(a) To come to compromise with someone
(b) Constant source of annoyance to someone
(c) To put someone at ease
(d) To desert someone in his/her difficulties

7. To play second fiddle
(a) To be happy, cheerful and healthy
(b) To be subordinate in position
(c) To promote
(d) To remain on top

8. To keep the ball rolling
(a) To earn more and more
(b) To work constantly
(c) To keep the conversation going
(d) To make the best use of

9. A storm in a tea-cup
(a) Unexpected event
(b) A danger signal
(c) Much excitement over something trivial
(d) A great noise

10. To have something up one's sleeve
(a) A grand idea
(b) A secret plan
(c) A profitable plan
(d) Something important

Directions (Q. Nos. 11-22) Given below are set of sentences where in each sentence an idiom has been used. Options of meaning are given below the sentence. Choose the best option for the meaning.

11. Everybody thought Jane and Tim were a happy couple, but it was all just make believe.
(a) Modesty (b) Pretending
(c) Reality (d) Denial

12. Man's first walk on the moon made History.
(a) Was forgotten
(b) Was unheard of
(c) Was meaningful enough to influence History
(d) Is only talked in History books

13. You can make people's day just by telling them how important they are to you.
(a) Displease people
(b) Resent people
(c) Give people great pleasure
(d) Antipathise people

14. He was thrown out of the company as he was fond of taking French Leave too often.
(a) Long absence
(b) Leave on the pretext of illness
(c) Casual leave
(d) Leave without permission

15. I am ambitious and do not want to rest on my laurels.
(a) Be dissatisfied (b) Be happy
(c) Be complace (d) Be relaxed

16. Things are progressing well-don't do anything to rock the boat.
(a) Create difficulties
(b) Conspire against
(c) Upset the balance
(d) Agitate against

17. The model's conference was a golden opportunity for me to sell my beauty products.
(a) A chance to win gold
(b) A chance to meet some VIP
(c) The perfect chance
(d) The favourite moment

18. Writing personal e-mails in the office is a grey area that needs to be discussed at the next meeting.
(a) A dark area
(b) Unlighted
(c) Something without a rule or answer
(d) Objectionable matter

19. I am green with envy over Julia's promotion to the new post of manager in the company.
(a) Delighted
(b) Very jealous
(c) Full of enmity
(d) Angry

20. When relatives come to town my grandmother rolls out the red carpet.
(a) Spreads red carpet
(b) Treat someone like royalty
(c) Treat shabbily or improperly
(d) Treat formally

21. I always have the blues during the winter time.
(a) Feel unhappy
(b) Happy
(c) Feel sad or depressed
(d) Feel anxious

22. We told Grandma that her cake was delicious, which was actually a white lie.

(a) A total lie

(b) Wrong lie

(c) An innocent lie to protect another person's feeling

(d) An intentional lie

Directions (Q. Nos. 23-36) Fill in the blanks with appropriate phrasal verb from the given options.

23. The police .... the robbery of a famous painting.

(a) are finding in (b) are looking into

(c) are finding out (d) are looking on

24. We had to .... the trip because of the bad weather.

(a) call out (b) take off

(c) call off (d) put off

25. After 20 years together Paul and Julia .... (end up a relationship).

(a) broke away (b) broke down

(c) split up (d) split off

26. It's your problem, so try to .... it ....

(a) solve, in (b) sort, out

(c) work, in (d) sort, off

27. This horrible weather .... me .... (depress).

(a) gets, down (b) works, down

(c) puts, down (d) breaks, down

28. What does this word mean? I'll .... it .... in the dictionary.

(a) look, for

(b) look, out

(c) look, in

(d) look, up

29. Don't smoke in the forest. Fires .... easily at this time of the year.

(a) breaks in

(b) break out

(c) breaks up

(d) broke in

30. Your website has helped me a lot to .... the good work.

(a) keep up (b) keep in

(c) keep of (d) keep out

31. I've missed many lessons, so now I'll have to .... the other students.

(a) look up (b) catch up with

(c) hurry up (d) put up

32. It is too cold in here. Shall I .... the heating?

(a) turn up (b) turn on

(c) turn down (d) None of these

33. The car .... in the middle of the motor way.

(a) break away (b) broke up

(c) broke down (d) break up

34. Harish always trying to .... an unpleasant task.

(a) get into

(b) get out of

(c) get down

(d) get away

35. It is no good .... from your problems.

(a) running into

(b) running out

(c) running away

(d) running down

36. I must go to the shop. We've .... of food.

(a) run out (b) run away

(c) run with (d) run over

2 Marks Questions

37. Match the following phrasal verbs to their meanings.

Column A	Column B
A. Ask around	1. Forcibly enter
B. Break down	2. Cancel
C. Break into	3. Ask many people the same questions
D. Break out	4. stop functioning
E. Call off	5. Escape

Codes

	A	B	C	D	E
(a)	3	1	4	5	2
(b)	3	1	5	4	2
(c)	3	4	1	5	2
(d)	4	3	1	2	5

38. Identify the pair which is incorrectly matched.

A	B
A. See eye to eye	agreeing with someone
B. When pigs fly	something that will never happen
C. A piece of cake	something very difficult
D. Break a leg	good luck

(a) Only A (b) Both A and B
(c) Only D (d) Only C

39. Replace the underlined word with the correct idiom or phrase.

1. A video call from my favourite film star on my birthday was a complete <u>surprise</u>.

A. A damp squib
B. Bolt from the blue
C. A field day
D. A mare's nest

(a) Only A
(b) Only B
(c) Both B and C
(d) Both A and D

40. Choose the sentence with the correct usage of idioms.

1. By working part-time and looking after her kids two days a week, she managed to get the best of both worlds.
2. They finally saw eye to eye on the business deal.
3. By taking my dad on holiday, I let the cat out of the bag. I got to go away but also spend time with him.
4. Fuel these days costs a piece of cake.

Codes

(a) Only 1 (b) Both 1 and 2
(c) Both 3 and 4 (d) 1, 2 and 4

41. Choose the sentence with the incorrect usage of idioms.

1. The subject of bullying and fighting in my school is a hot potato.
2. Learning English is a piece of cake as long as you do it using our website.
3. I go to visit my grandfather only once in a blue moon; he lives in a remote farm house.
4. Hey Jack! You're always playing angel's advocate! Give it a rest and mind your own business.

Codes

(a) 2 and 3 (b) 1, 3 and 4
(c) Only 4 (d) None of these

42. Choose the sentence with correct usage of idioms.

1. The idiom 'miss the boat' means 'miss the chance'.
2. The idiom 'zip your lip' means 'to stop talking'.

Codes

(a) Only 1 is correct
(b) Only 2 is correct
(c) Both 1 and 2 are correct
(d) Neither 1 nor 2 are correct

Chapter 12

Cloze Test

1 Mark Questions

Directions (Q. Nos. 1-5) In the following passage, there are blanks, each of which has been numbered. These numbers are printed below the passage and against each, four words/phrases are suggested, one of which fits the blank appropriately. Find out the appropriate word/phrase in each case.

The ......**(1)**....... of Bengal tigers left in the world has ......**(2)**...... from 100,000 to 4,000 over the last century. The main threats are ......**(3)**...... of habitat, poaching and the trade in tiger parts for Eastern medicines. Most Bengal tigers live in protected areas of India. Anti-poaching task-forces have been ......**(4)**...... up and there is also a trade ......**(5)**...... on tiger products in many countries, as a measure to save this rare species.

1. (a) form (b) kind (c) glory (d) number

2. (a) limited (b) shrunk (c) abolished (d) eliminated

3. (a) prevention (b) encroaching (c) condition (d) loss

4. (a) set (b) brought (c) swept (d) deployed

5. (a) agreement (b) contract (c) ban (d) link

Directions (Q. Nos. 6-10) In the following passage some of the words have been left out. Read the passage carefully and choose the correct word from the four alternatives to fill in the blanks.

The sun had set but there was still some light in the sky. Martin ......**(6)**....... on his elbow and looked ......**(7)**...... through the leaves. In the waters of the lake, close to the shore, he saw a ......**(8)**....... of alligators floating quietly. One of the creatures, ...**(9)**...... huge one, was lying on a high ......**(10)**...... of sand, a few yard from the water.

6. (a) sat (b) crossed (c) leaned (d) lay

7. (a) into (b) down (c) at (d) for

8. (a) semblance (b) family (c) volume (d) number

9. (a) an (b) a (c) one (d) single

10. (a) bank (b) peak (c) pit (d) pile

2 Marks Questions

Directions (Q. Nos. 11-16) In the following passage there are blanks, each of which has been numbered. These numbers are printed below the passage and against each, four words/phrases are suggested, one of which fits the blank appropriately. Find out the appropriate word/phrase in each case.

Once upon a time, Amarasakti ruled the city-state of Mahilaropyam in the South of India. He had three witless sons who became a matter of endless ....**(11)**.... for him. ....**(12)**..... that his sons had no interest in learning, the king summoned his ministers and said, "You know I am not happy with my sons. According to men of learning, an unborn son is better than a son who is a ....**(13)**.... A son who is stupid will bring dishonour to his father. How can I make my sons fit to be my ....**(14)**.... ? I turn to you for advice." One of the ministers ....**(15)**.... the name of Vishnu Sharman, a great scholar enjoying the ....**(16)**.... of hundreds of his disciples.

11. (a) ache (b) worry (c) joy (d) pity

12. (a) Fact (b) Belief (c) Since (d) Realising

13. (a) stupid (b) brilliant (c) fool (d) uneducated

14. (a) self (b) place (c) successors (d) level

15. (a) suggested (b) requested (c) called (d) pointed

16. (a) teachings (b) attendance (c) glamour (d) respect

Directions (Q. Nos. 17-22) In the following passage, there are blanks, each of which has been numbered. These numbers are printed below the passage and against each, four words/phrases are suggested, one of which fits the blank appropriately. Find out the appropriate word/phrase in each case. Prior to independence the healthcare sector in India was in ....**(17)**.... with a large number of deaths and rampant spread of infectious diseases. After independence the Government of India laid ....**(18)**..... on primary healthcare and India has put in sustained efforts to better the healthcare system ....**(19)**..... the country. The government initiative was not enough to meet the demands of a growing population be it in primary, secondary or tertiary healthcare. Alternate sources of finance were critical for the sustainability of the health sector.

Till about 20 years ago, private sector ventures in the healthcare sector ....**(20)**..... of only solo practitioners, small hospitals and nursing homes. The quality of service provided was excellent especially in the hospitals run by charitable trusts and religious foundations. In 1980's realising that the government on its own would not be able to ....**(21)**..... for healthcare, the government allowed the entry of private sector to reduce the ....**(22)**.... between supply and demand for healthcare.

17. (a) shambles (b) failure (c) demand (d) prosperity

18. (a) bricks (b) emphasise (c) request (d) stress

19. (a) through (b) across (c) sharing (d) with

20. (a) made (b) comprise (c) consisted (d) is

21. (a) cater (b) provide (c) manage (d) survive

22. (a) gap (b) position (c) distance (d) length

Chapter 13

Reading Comprehension

1 Mark Questions

Directions (Q. Nos. 1-5) Read the following passage carefully and answer the questions that follow by selecting the most appropriate option.

Travel for Next Year

(a) Here are some key trends that will 'define' tourism in India this year, which promises to be very interesting for the tourism industry and travellers, both Foreign and Indian.

(b) One, consumers will continue to seek travel deals, low airfares, last minute bookings, 5 star hotels at 4 star prices, etc. Using the 'discovering power' of the internet, more and more consumers will demonstrate 'smart buying behaviour'.

(c) Two, we will continue to 'mature' as travellers, seeking unique and memorable travel experiences, be it adventure tourism, wildlife tourism or quest for exotic destinations.

(d) Three, the use of the internet and other technology will increase whether it is trip planning (where we will increasingly use the net to plan trips based on insights and advice from other travellers), the trip booking, the trip itself (where we will be exposed to technologies such as GPS, Wi-Fi in trains, aircraft, airports, etc) or in the post-trip stage (where we will use the net to share photographs on websites like Facebook, etc.), we will adopt technology as never before.

(e) Four, some other trends are: Goa remains the undisputed destination of choice. 'Staycations' emerge as a 'mini-trend' with people deciding to stay at home rather than spend money on travelling.

1. According to the author, smart buying behaviour means

(a) using the internet to buy things.

(b) getting the best deals with the help of the internet.

(c) using money wisely.

(d) discovering the power of the internet.

2. In which areas related to travel, use of internet and other technology will be on increase?

(a) Trip planning and trip booking.

(b) Our actual trip.

(c) Post trip stage (sharing photograph at social media with the help of internet).

(d) All of the above

3. The author has invented the word 'staycation' to mean

(a) preferring to stay in other people's home for vacation.

(b) preferring to stay indoor during summer vacation instead of going out.

(c) preferring to stay at home during holidays.

(d) preferring to stay at home instead of travelling to save money.

4. The author believes that in coming years,

(a) the internet and technology will become mandatory in travel.

(b) the internet and technology will be used for planning trips.

(c) the internet and technology will enhance travel experience.

(d) the internet and technology will be adopted for the first time.

5. The word 'exotic' means

(a) tropical and sub-tropical

(b) foreign and native

(c) unusual and exciting

(d) far and wide

Directions (Q. Nos. 6-10) Read the passage carefully and answer the questions that follow.

(1) **Muturkham (Jharkhand), 15th January, 2012** Eleven years ago, Muturkham forests, lying South-East of capital Ranchi, used to be the timber mafia's busy workplace. No different from the rest of the state, which has lost 50% of forest cover to illegal logging in the last 10 years. Until 1999, when Muturkham's jungle mafia met 'Lady Tarzan'.

(2) Jamuna Tuddu, 32, a short and stout woman belonging to the Santhal tribe who had studied till Class X, led a band of 25 tribal housewives to form the Van Suraksha Samiti (Forest Protection Committee) and registered it with the State Forest Department. The women patrolled the forests in three groups: collared illegal loggers, usually hired hands from nearby villages - and handed them over to the Forest Department. Word spread that the trees in Muturkham were not to be touched. The 50-hectares forest in East Singhbhum district which had turned barren (the mafia had chopped down every tree over 3 metres tall) now has 1 lakh trees. There is a kendu, eucalyptus or acacia tree every 6 feet; the gap between two trees 10 years ago used to be more than 24 feet. Several species of reptiles and avians, wild boars, hare and the elephant, have made this forest their home.

(3) The local initiative could well be the model for protecting the 23,60,500 hectares of Jharkhand's rich jungle cover - the size of about 16 Delhis - from timber cartels.

(4) Tuddu has worked as a mason as well as a beautician to supplement the family income. Her reasons for forming this committee were prompted by basic economics: there was no firewood in her kitchen.

(5) In the summers, there was no shade. "We had no firewood, no fodder for our cattle and water levels were dipping across a 15 km area" she says. "Today, anyone caught felling trees is fined ` 501 and handed over to the Forest Department." The amount is deposited in the Samiti's fund,

utilised for community welfare work and to purchase cell phones for better networking during patrols.

(6) Muturkham has been rewarded for its brave enterprise. A smooth road connects it with the Chakulia- Tata Main Road and an overhead water tank ensures 24-hours supply to every household. There is a well and a check dam on a hill stream. There is a school building, a generator set and machines to make leaf plates.

(7) Most of these were delivered by the Forest Department as a gesture of thanks for the Samiti's achievements under the World Food Programme and the Mahatma Gandhi National Rural Employment Guarantee Scheme.

(8) Tuddu, however, does not rest on her laurels. It is 6 am and 'Lady Tarzan' as she is locally known, is tightening the strings of her bow in her house. A group of around 12 women, some with children in their arms, quietly assemble outside, each carrying traditional weapons and lathis for the daily patrol. Tuddu leads them to the Muturkham forests, quite fearlessly.

(9) Tuddu's women say their forest duties do not affect their household and farming responsibilities. The village head, Charu Charan Tuddu says, "The entire village is in their debt and thanks to the committee, Muturkham women feel empowered."

6. Two qualities of Jamuna Tuddu's personality are
(a) aggressive and temperamental
(b) brave and fearless
(c) resourceful and determined
(d) housewife, teacher

7. Van Suraksha Samiti was formed with the aim of
(a) save the wildlife.
(b) not allowing anyone to enter the area.
(c) save the trees from being felled by mafia.
(d) to provide employment to women.

8. Due to the efforts of Jamuna Tuddu, the Muturkham forest area has which of the following?
(a) a smooth road connects it.
(b) an overhead water tank supplies 24 hours water in the area.
(c) a school building and a generator set.
(d) All of the above

9. Which of the following is a synonym of word 'felling' used in fifth paragraph?
(a) Going down
(b) Grow more trees
(c) Cutting mercilessly
(d) Feeling bad

10. The Idiom 'To rest on her laurels' in eight paragraph means
(a) take rest for long hours.
(b) to sleep peacefully.
(c) to feel satisfied with your achievement.
(d) to be careful not to lose the success.

2 Marks Questions

Directions (Q. Nos. 11-15) Read the passage carefully and answer the questions that that follow by choosing the most appropriate option.

So, You Want To Be A Cartoonist ?

What writers struggle to express through numerous newspaper columns, the cartoon manages in a pointed one-liner. Little wonder then, that the first thing most of us like to see when we pick up a newspaper is the cartoon. Simple though it may seem, making a cartoon is an art that requires a combination of hard work, training and a good sense of humour. Cartoonists say that the cartoons that make us laugh the most are in fact the cartoons that are hardest to make. Even celebrated cartoonists like RK Laxman admits that making a cartoon is not a piece of cake. Laxman says he has to wait for over six hours, which includes spending a lot of time scanning newspapers and television channels before any idea strikes him.

So, how does one become a cartoonist? Which of us has the talent to make it? How can we master the rib-tickling strokes and the witty one-liners? How can we make people smile or laugh? There are few colleges or schools for cartoonists. Most cartoonists come from art colleges, while some learn the craft on their own. Most established cartoonists are of the view that no institute can teach you to make a cartoon. "You can pick up the craft, you may learn to sketch and draw in institutes, but no one can teach anyone how to make a good cartoon," says Uday Shankar, a cartoonist with Navbharat Times. While basics, like drawing and sketching can be learnt in an art college, and are important skills, these alone, do not make a good cartoonist. Because it's a question of one's creativity and sense of humour; two qualities one simply may not have. The advice established cartoonists give is that just because you can sketch, don't take it for granted that you will become a cartoonist.

11. What, according to Laxman, is the challenge in creating a good cartoon?

(a) Waiting for the right thought.

(b) Browsing newspapers to emerge and television.

(c) Getting the right kind of information.

(d) Good drawing and sketching training skills.

12. Which of these words best describe the passage?

(a) Humorous (b) Technical

(c) Challenging (d) Informative

13. 'Don't take it for granted' – choose the option that is closest in meaning.

(a) Don't assume that you will.

(b) Don't hope that you will become a cartoonist.

(c) Don't believe that you will.

(d) Don't imagine that you will become a cartoonist.

14. The word 'scanning' would mean

(a) scrutinise.
(b) to look carefully and quickly.
(c) to pass light over a document or picture in computer.
(d) All of the above

15. Of the many qualities that a cartoonist should have, which of the following is not referred to directly, but can be inferred from the passage?

(a) Knowledge of current affairs
(b) Knowledge of educational technologies
(c) Knowledge of news
(d) Knowledge of different current affairs and languages

Directions (Q. Nos. 16-20) Read the poem carefully and answer the questions by choosing the right answer from the given options.

Patriotism

Breathes there the man with soul so dead,
Who never to himself hath said,
"This is my own, my native land!"
Whose heart hath ne'er within him burned
As home his footsteps he hath turned
From wandering on a foreign strand?

If such there breathe, go, mark him well;
For him no Minstrel raptures swell;

High though his titles, proud his name, Boundless his wealth as wish can claim;
Despite those titles, power, and pelf,

The wretch, concentred all in self,
Living, shall forfeit fair renown,
And, doubly dying, shall go down
To the vile dust from whence he sprung,
Unwept, unhonoured, and unsung.

— By Sir Walter Scott

16. The poet's main idea in the poem is

(a) those who become rich must hate their country.
(b) travelling abroad helps a person to appreciate home.
(c) those who do not love their country, will not be honoured.
(d) patriotism is the last refuge for scoundrels.

17. What does the poet mean by the expression 'such people will be double dying'?

(a) They will not die alone.
(b) They will die physically and also be forgotten.
(c) Their death will be painful.
(d) They will die, then rise again.

18. What is the most likely meaning of the word 'pelf' used in the poem ?

(a) Power (b) Wealth
(c) Stealth (d) Health

19. One can infer from the poem that Sir Walter Scott

(a) loved his homeland
(b) was from Great Britain
(c) hated war
(d) spoke many languages

20. What does the word 'concentred' most likely mean?

(a) Swirling or curved
(b) Arrogant, proud
(c) Focused on, concerned with
(d) Looking upward

Directions (Q. Nos. 21-25) Read the poem carefully and answer the questions by choosing the right answer from the given options.

A Narrow Fellow in the Grass

A narrow fellow in the grass
Occasionally rides—
You may have met him—did you not
His notice sudden is—
The grass divides as with a comb—
A spotted shaft is seen—
And then it closes at your feet
And opens further on—
He likes a Boggy Acre—
A floor too cool for corn—
Yet when a boy, and barefoot—
I more than once at noon
Have passed, I thought, a whiplash
Unbraiding in the Sun
When, stooping to secure it,
It wrinkled, and was gone—
Several of nature's people
I know, and they know me—
feel for them a transport
Of cordiality—
But never met this fellow,
Attended, or alone—
Without a tighter breathing
And zero at the bone—

21. 'Who' or 'what' is the fellow in the poem?

(a) A whiplash (b) A snake
(c) A gust of wind (d) A boy

22. The phrase 'without a tighter-breathing' most nearly indicates

(a) fright (b) cold
(c) grief (d) awe

23. The phrase 'nature's people' means

(a) nature lovers
(b) children
(c) animals
(d) neighbours

24. The expression 'transport of cordiality' here, would mean

(a) walking in a car.
(b) friendly with some animals.
(c) feeling of knowing each other.
(d) fear for these animals.

25. The speaker of this poem is most likely

(a) an adult woman
(b) an adult man
(c) Emily Dickenson, the poetess
(d) a young boy

Directions (Q. Nos. 26-30) Read the poem carefully and answer the questions by choosing the right answer from the given options.

The Lapwing

In the dark that falls before the dawn,
When the dew has settled on the thorn,
When the stars have been obscured by clouds, A silence covers all things in shrouds.

No wind sighs in the mulberry tree,
No firefly glimmers wild and free,
A shadow has wrapped the night in gloom,
It's silent as a deserted tomb.

All of a sudden a lapwing's cry
Cuts the black silence as it flies by,
Again and again it slashes the dark
That haunts the empty, desolate park.

Anguish, sorrow pours from its throat,
It wings in the night, note after note;

I open my window so the light
Will flood the dark of this wretched night.

Why does it cry so miserably?
Why is it so solitary?
All I know is that loss and ache
Are left behind in the lapwing's wake.

26. What happens when darkness falls? There is
(a) complete silence everywhere.
(b) a shroud covering all things.
(c) the cry of the lapwing to be heard.
(d) gloom and desolation.

27. When does the lapwing come out?
(a) At dawn
(b) At night
(c) Just before dawn
(d) In the morning

28. The expression 'stars been obscured by clouds' would mean
(a) not able to see stars due to clouds.
(b) stars shining between the clouds.
(c) starless sky due to clouds.
(d) stars shining in spite of cloudy weather.

29. The poet opens the window so that
(a) he can get some light.
(b) he can hear the lapwing.
(c) he can see the lapwing.
(d) he can get some air.

30. We can infer from the poem that lapwing is miserable because of
(a) loneliness and glood
(b) loss and pain
(c) darkness and loss
(d) darkness and pain

Chapter 14

Writing Skills

1 Mark Questions

Directions (Q. Nos. 1-7) The given notice is written by Secretary of Gymkhana Club, Madurai, to inform the members to attend an extra ordinary meeting of the governing body. It included all relevant details like date, time, venue and purpose of the meeting. Sign as Prabhu/Pratibha. Some blanks are given which are numbered. Choose the correct word from the options given and complete the notice.

.......**(1)**.......

NOTICE

10th October, 20XX

.......**(2)**........

All the members are hereby informed that there ......**(3)**...... an extraordinary meeting of the governing body on Friday, 16th October, 2014 at 9:30 a.m. at the ......**(4)**...... of the ....**(5)**...... Club. The meeting ......**(6)**...... called to decide the Chief Guest for the Annual Day Programme of the club. ....**(7)**...... is mandatory.

Pratibha/Prabhu
(Secretary)

1. (a) Salutation
(b) Name of event
(c) Both (a) and (b)
(d) Name of governing body

2. (a) Meeting of the Club Members
(b) Meeting of the Governing Body
(c) Meeting
(d) Meeting of All Members

3. (a) will be (b) has to be
(c) is going to be (d) would be

4. (a) club (b) board room
(c) office (d) residence

5. (a) Chairman (b) Secretary
(c) Governor (d) President

6. (a) has been (b) had been
(c) have been (d) is being

7. (a) Presence (b) Attendance
(c) Signature (d) Coming

Directions (Q. Nos. 8-16) Your school has planned an excursion to Lonavala, near Mumbai during the autumn holidays. Write a notice in not more than 50 words for your school notice board, giving detailed information and inviting the names of those who are desirous to join. Sign as Naresh/Namita, Head Boy/Girl DAV English School, Bandra, Mumbai.

The notice is given below with some parts missing which are numbered. Options are given for each numbered word or phrase. Choose the correct option.

.......**(8)**........ Bandra, Mumbai

NOTICE

10th October, 20XX

.......**(9)**.......

The school ......**(10)**...... an excursion to Lonavala during the autumn-break from 22nd October to 27th October, 2021 for the students of class XI and XII. ......**(11)**...... the trip is ₹ 1000/- per student. Interested students may ......**(12)**...... their names to the undersigned by 14th October 2021, alongwith ......**(13)**...... letter from their parents or ......**(14)**...... For more information contact the ......**(15)**......

Naresh/Namita

.....**(16)**.....

8. (a) Name of school (b) Name of event
(c) Salutation (d) Both (a) and (c)

9. (a) Excursion to Khandala
(b) Excursion to Lonavala
(c) Picnic to Bengaluru
(d) Trip to Pune

10. (a) has been planning
(b) has planned
(c) is planning
(d) is going to plan

11. (a) The expenses of
(b) The cost of
(c) Money needed for
(d) Any of these

12. (a) give (b) submit
(c) surrender (d) write

13. (a) Ok (b) permission
(c) consent (d) letter

14. (a) teacher incharge
(b) guardians
(c) family
(d) parents

15. (a) principal
(b) undersigned
(c) staff secretary
(d) tour incharge

16. (a) Head Boy/Head Girl
(b) Head Boy
(c) Prefect
(d) Monitor

17. The content of a letter from you to your father is given in four blanks which should be filled by statements PQRS. Choose the correct answer from the options given.

24, Subhash Hostel,
Chandigarh
9th October, 20XX

Dear Daddy,

I received your letter today in the morning. You asked me ....**(ii)**.... poor marks in English paper.

First of all, I would like to tell you that I put very hard labour in English.

As you are aware that I am not good at Grammar, So I couldn't attend the Grammar portion so well. .....**(ii)** ..., So I have talked to my English teacher who has consented to give me tuitions for two months only. Without good command over English Grammar, ... **(iii)**..... in English. Please allow me to take English tuition, so that I will be able to overcome my shortcomings in English language.

In other subjects, daddy, I have secured more than 88% marks, but in English I know .....**(iv)**..... I assure of hard work and better result in future.

Convey my regards to Mom and Grand Ma.

Yours lovingly

Ajay

Options

(P) it is not possible to secure good marks

(Q) I have performed very badly

(R) the reason of securing

(S) I need tuition/extra coaching in English Grammar

Choose your answer from the given options.

(a) QRSP (b) RSPQ

(c) RQPS (d) SRQP

Directions (Q. Nos. 18-23) Content of letter to editor about the ill-treatment meted out to stray dogs at the hands of callous and indifferent people is given below.

You will find some numbered blanks. Options of them are given the letter. Fill up the blanks using the appropriate option.

26, WEA Karol Bagh,
New Delhi.
11th October, 20XX
The Editor,
The Hindu
KG Marg,
New Delhi-110001

Subject: ....**(18)**.......

Sir,

Through the columns of your esteemed newspaper, I ....**(19)**....... of the concerned authorities towards the ill-treatment meted out to stray dogs by indifferent people.

I feel greatly distressed and disturbed at the manner in which stray dogs are being treated by people who live in my locality. Starving homeless dogs are chased away instead of ....**(20)**........ homes to them. Many of them become victims of fatal accidents.

We need to protect stray dogs from ....**(21)**........ at the hands of human beings. We need to take care of the homeless stray dogs and provide them with a permanent home for life. The NGOs ....**(22)**....... to protect these animals. The common people should be more concerned towards these animals and do their ....**(23)**....... I hope the concerned authorities will take urgent steps to protect dogs from all kinds of cruelties meted out to them by the people.

Yours truly
Arun

18. (a) Cruelty towards stray dogs
(b) Loyalty towards stray dogs
(c) Stray dogs
(d) Problem of stray dogs

19. (a) want to bring into notice
(b) would like to bring into notice
(c) would like to state
(d) wanting to notice

20. (a) taking care
(b) giving shelter
(c) feeding and providing
(d) providing

21. (a) wrong people
(b) cruelty and suffering
(c) hunger and disease
(d) illness and torture

22. (a) must take care
(b) must come forward
(c) must promise to help them
(d) should promise

23. (a) best to protect the animals
(b) best to care about the stray dog
(c) best to feed and look after the stray dogs
(d) best possible care

Directions (Q. Nos. 24-32) Content of the report is given below related to organisation of an Inter School Quiz mentioning relevant details.

You will find some numbered blanks; options of them are given at the end of the report. Fill up the blanks by choosing the correct option.

GM Modi School, Modinagar
Inter School Quiz Contest
5th October, 2014

......**(24)**.......

Our school had the privilege of ......**(25)**....... this year's Inter School Quiz Contest. It was ....**(26)**....... on 25th September, 20XX in the school ......**(27)**........ The questions related to general ......**(28)**....... concerning 'alternative fuels' were asked. In all, eighteen ....**(29)**....... of three students each took part in it. First, preliminary ....**(30)**........ was held in which twelve questions were asked from each team. After preliminary round, six teams were selected for the final round. Sometimes, the questions were quite ....**(31)**........ but students showed their presence of mind, moreover it was team work which paid dividend in the end. It was a matter of ....**(32)**....... for us that our school team was declared the first prize winner. The chief guest and the principal congratulated the winners as well as the participants.

Ashish
X-A

24. (a) A Report (b) Notice
(c) Appeal (d) Article

25. (a) celebrating (b) organising
(c) holding (d) planting

26. (a) acted (b) held
(c) hold (d) celebrated

27. (a) ground (b) office
(c) auditorium (d) library

28. (a) reasoning (b) vocabulary
(c) knowledge (d) current affairs

29. (a) groups (b) teams
(c) members (d) leaders

30. (a) round (b) competition
(c) contest (d) None of these

31. (a) easy (b) problematic
(c) confusing (d) tricky

32. (a) glory (b) achievement
(c) pride (d) satisfaction

Direction (Q. No. 33-43) Content of a report written by tour guide of a company is given below related to tour to Leh area with is tourist when the coldburst and mudslide caused massive devastation in the area.

You will find some blanks in the report whose options are given below in box. Choose the correct option.

(i) sudden, (ii) caused, (iii) burst, (iv) located, (v) damaged, (vi) were, (vii) mudslide, (viii) blocked, (ix) stranded, (x) operational, (xi) work, (xii) survey, (xiii) makeshift

Cloud ....**(33)**....... caused Devastation in Leh

27th September, 2014

A Report

On 25th September, 20XX at 8 PM a ....**(34)**........ cloudburst and resulting mudslide in upper Leh region ....**(35)**........ massive devastation in the area.

A whole village Choglamsar .....(**36**)...... on the hillside got burried under the mass of mud.

In the upper part of Leh, houses were badly damaged. According to Government sources, around 200 people ....(**37**)........ reported dead. Around 1500 people were badly affected by the ....(**38**)....... as hotels and tourist lodges were badly damaged due to excessive water. All the roads were ....(**39**)........ by debris making so many people ....(**40**)....... .

The Chief Minister made an aerial ......(**41**)...... of the area. He said that rescue ....(**42**)........ was likely to start within 48 hours. Local people were taking the injured to nearby hospital. The airport and roads could be made ....(**43**)........ by Saturday for military planes. Compensation of ₹ 1 lakh has been announced by the Chief Minister to the Kith 2 km of the dead.

33. (a) (vi) (b) (ii)
(c) (iii) (d) (viii)

34. (a) (iv) (b) (i)
(c) (vi) (d) (ix)

35. (a) (ii) (b) (iii)
(c) (vii) (d) (x)

36. (a) (vii) (b) (xii)
(c) (iv) (d) (ix)

37. (a) (viii) (b) (vi)
(c) (xi) (d) (v)

38. (a) (vii) (b) (iii)
(c) (xii) (d) (xiii)

39. (a) (viii) (b) (x)
(c) (xi) (d) (ix)

40. (a) (x) (b) (viii)
(c) (ix) (d) (vi)

41. (a) (xi) (b) (xii)
(c) (x) (d) (vii)

42. (a) (xi) (b) (ii)
(c) (vi) (d) (i)

43. (a) (iii) (b) (v)
(c) (x) (d) (xiii)

2 Marks Questions

Directions (Q. Nos. 44-46) Diary entry is given below sharing a experience of the journey from home to railway station. You will find the some blank in it. Fill in the blanks with help of options given below.

19th January, 2021

Monday

9 PM

Dear Diary,

Today I ...(**44**)... to Bangalore railway station, Yeshwantpura, to receive my uncle and aunt who ...(**45**)... from Mumbai. It was a bright sunny day. Sun was shining like a star. While my father and I were crossing the Orion mall, we ...(**46**)... three elephants that reminded me of my Kerala trip.

Last year I went on a Kerala trip, where we visited around 5 cities like Cochin, Wayanad, Munnar, Kovalam, and Alappuzha. All the places were really awesome and beautiful. Then we went to Elephant junction Thekkady, Kumily, where people go for elephant rides. I rode sitting above the elephant around for 2 and half hours. Then we have also done elephant bath and feeding. We took a lot of pictures with elephants. It was a nice trip and I still can't get over it.

Vikram

44. (a) gone (b) was going
(c) went (d) have gone

45. (a) had come (b) were coming
(c) are coming (d) came

46. (a) saw (b) had seen
(c) had been seen (d) was seeing

Directions (Q. Nos. 47-49) Read the following telephone conversation that took place between the salesman of an electrical appliances shop and an unsatisfied customer. The manager is away from the shop. The salesman leaves a message for him. Write the message using not more than 50 words.

Message

Customer : Hello! Is this Taj Electrical Appliances?

Salesman : Yes, Madam. What can I do for you?

Customer : I've got a problem with the hairdryer that I bought last week.

Salesman : I'm sorry to hear that. What is the problem?

Customer : Well, first of all, I ordered it two months ago but I received it only last week. Secondly, I find it useless.

Salesman : Does it work?

Customer : It doesn't dry my hair. When I switch it on, it just goes 'buzzzzz' but it does not get hot at all.

Salesman : Madam, I apologize. We'll be happy to replace the dryer for you. Or we'll give you a refund instead.

Customer : Oh, great! I'd like a refund then.

Message

22 March, 20xx
5:30 p.m.
Sir,
An .....**(47)**..... customer who bought a hairdryer last week rang up. She said she .....**(48)**..... it two months ago but received it only last week. Secondly, she found it useless as it does not dry her hair.
She .....**(49)**..... for a refund.
Ram Gopal

47. (a) interesting (b) angry
(c) happy (d) dissatisfied

48. (a) had ordered
(b) ordered
(c) had been ordered
(d) would have ordered

49. (a) has ordered
(b) has fought
(c) has asked
(d) has threatened

Directions (Q. Nos. 50-52) Given below an advertisement for 'Situation Vacant' column of a local daily with some blank in it. Complete the advertisement with help of the options given below.

Situation vacant

.....**(50)**..... an efficient, smart and hardworking data .....**(51)**..... operator for a leading manufacturing company in Gurgaon. Qualifications – Graduate, age 20-35 years. Typing speed 50 w.p.m. Preference to those who have 1-2 years of experience. Salary upto INR 260000 annually. Apply with .....**(52)**..... resume. within 15 days to ABC Ltd., Sector 30, Gurgaon.

50. (a) Wants
(b) Is wanting
(c) Has been wanted
(d) Wanted

51. (a) exit (b) entry
(c) management (d) creating

52. (a) updated (b) updating
(c) update (d) updates

Directions (Q. Nos. 53-55) The debate on banning the use of animals in the laboratories for the purpose of dissection is given below. Some blanks are given which are numbered. Fill in the blanks with the help of options given below.

Learning zoology will never be the same. There will be no frog, mouse or guinea pig to dissect in laboratories. I,Arunita, support the government's decision to ban the use of animals for the purpose of dissection in laboratories.

The indiscriminate removal of these animals from their .....**(53)**..... habitats has disrupted the biodiversity and ecological balance. The case of frogs, the population of which has declined to alarming levels in recent times, is often cited as an example. Institutions have .....**(54)**..... to follow the laws and guidelines about animals and their welfare, therefore, the government was forced to impose this ban. Also, I feel students should be taught to be compassionate towards animals and this can be an effective step in this direction. Laboratory exercises should make use of museum specimens, photographs, video clippings, models, charts and field operations. The only thing that an animal dissection lab teaches students is that an animal's life is .....**(55)**..... . Students can definitely learn about animals and how their bodies work without taking apart its insides. So, I may conclude by saying that I am in complete agreement with the government's decision to ban the use of animals for dissection.

53. (a) natural (b) artificial
(c) normal (d) forest

54. (a) not (b) failed
(c) succeeded (d) fail

55. (a) disposable and unimportant
(b) precious and important
(c) easy and comfortable
(d) None of the above

Chapter 15

Communication Skills

1 Mark Questions

Directions (Q. Nos. 1-3) The following is a conversation between Dheeraj Chopra and the Secretary of International Computers. Dheeraj wishes to speak to Sanjay Bhatnagar, but the latter is not available on the line. Dheeraj leaves his message for Mr Bhatnagar to the Secretary. On the basis of this telephonic conversation, answer the following question choosing the correct option.

SECRETARY	International Computers, Good morning.
DHEERAJ	Good morning. Can I speak to Sanjay Bhatnagar in the Sales Department? I am Dheeraj Chopra from Chopra Electronics.
SECRETARY	Just a moment, please. (She tries Sales Deptt., but no answer). Hello, Mr Chopra, I am afraid, Mr Bhatnagar is in a meeting. Can I take a message?
DHEERAJ	Yes, please .... could you ask Mr Bhatnagar to ring me up immediately. It is about our order of 10 core *i*-7 processor computers. Mr Bhatnagar had promised to deliver it last week but I haven't received even a single machine so far. Ask Mr Bhatnagar to deliver the computers in three days, otherwise, I'm afraid, I will have to cancel the order.
SECRETARY	Ok Sir, I'll give him your message. I'm sure he'll get in touch with you as soon as the meeting is over. Thank you for calling.
DHEERAJ	Thank you. Bye

1. State the reason of Mr Chopra calling International Computers.

(a) Mr Chopra wanted to fix an appointment with MD.
(b) Mr Chopra wanted to talk about the payment schedule with the Accounts Department.
(c) Mr Chopra wanted to speak to Mr Sanjay Bhatnagar of Sales Department.
(d) Mr Chopra wanted to discuss a project.

2. What issue did Mr Chopra want to discuss with Mr Bhatnagar?

(a) It was about a new project.
(b) It was about the delay in the delivery of 10-core i-7 processor computers.
(c) It was about the payment details.
(d) It was about non-receipt of documents sent by Mr Bhatnagar.

3. What action would Mr Chopra take in case of undue delay in delivery of computers?

(a) Stop all dealings with the company
(b) Stop payment
(c) Cancel the order
(d) Complaint to the seniors

Directions (Q. Nos. 4-6) On the basis of this telephonic conversation, given below is the message in approximately 50 words. Fill in the blanks with the help of options which are given for each numbered word. Choose the correct option.

Message

Mr Dheeraj Chopra of Chopra Electronics rang up. He ...**(4)**... about the non-delivery of 10 core i-7 processor computers ...**(5)**... to be sent last week. If order will not be delivered in next three days, Mr Chopra may ...**(6)**... the order.

4. (a) discussed (b) praised
(c) complained (d) shouted

5. (a) pledged (b) promised
(c) assured (d) agreed

6. (a) stop (b) postpone
(c) renew (d) cancel

Directions (Q. Nos. 7-9) On the basis of this telephonic conversation given below answer the following questions. Choose the appropriate option.

Telephonic Conversation with Message

Listen All | Person A | Person B

A "Hello? This is Steve."

B "Hi Steve! This is Mary from ABC Company. I'm returning your call."

A "Hi Mary! How are you doing?"

B "I'm doing great, thanks."

A "Thanks for returning my call. I couldn't figure out why the closing balance on fiscal year 2003 didn't match the opening balance of 2004."

B "When I checked, it was matching. How much is the difference?"

A "The amount is exactly $ 42,000."

B "Oh! I know what the problem is. We opened another bank account at the end of fiscal year 2003. I might not have included the new bank statements when I sent over the information."

B "That makes sense. I'm just glad it wasn't out of my miscalculation. Can you send over the statements? It should be done by end of day since everything looks good."

B "Sure. I'll fax them to you immediately. Is 555-123-4567 the number I should fax it to?"

A "Yes. That is the correct number."

B "I will do it right now."

A "Thank you for your help."

B "I should have sent them over to you the first time. I apologise for that."

A "No problem."

B "Thank you."

A "Thank you. Bye."

7. Mr Steve called up ABC company because

(a) Mr Steve wanted to discuss the discrepancy in the balance sheet.
(b) Mr Steve wanted to talk to somebody from Sales Department.
(c) He wanted to fix up an appointment with the Director of ABC Company.
(d) Mr Steve complained about non-matching of balance of 2003 and 2004.

8. The phrase "I am returning your call" will mean

(a) somebody called and you are answering the call.
(b) telephone someone who has given you a message.

(c) telephone someone who tried to telephone you earlier.
(d) telephone someone to order some items.

9. What was the explanation provided by Mary to Mr Steve?
(a) There was a miscalculation.
(b) New bank statements were not added.
(c) There was a printing error.
(d) Non-inclusion of previous balance.

Directions (Q. Nos. 10-12) Given below is a message based on this telephonic conversation. Choose the correct option and fill in the blanks.

Message

Mary of ABC Company returned a call to ...**(10)**.... Steve who asked the reason of non-matching of ...**(11)**... in balance sheets of 2003-04. She informed him that it was due to opening of a new bank account and non ...**(12)**... of it at the time of the sending information.

Options

10. (a) customer (b) client
(c) vendor (d) chairman

11. (a) numbers (b) amount
(c) balance (d) money

12. (a) matching (b) mixing
(c) inclusion (d) entry

Directions (Q. Nos. 13-16) Choose the most appropriate options to complete the following dialogue with the help of options given below.

Write the correct answer in the answer sheet against the correct blank number.

Niharika: Hi Dad. I'm in trouble - I'm in a restaurant and someone ......**(13)** ...... my bag. I don't know what to do.

Her father: Oh..... Have you called the police?

Niharika: No. I don't know if I .....**(14)**.....

Her father: You can ask the restaurant manager to call them.

Niharika: OK, I will do that. I .....**(15)**..... my keys and my money. Worse, I am worried that the people in the restaurant won't believe me. Could you come over and help me?

Her father: I am really sorry. I am quite busy now. I have to make a presentation in about ten minutes. I ....**(16)**..... your Mum.

13. (a) is stealing; (b) has stolen
(c) has been stolen (d) is stolen

14. (a) would (b) should
(c) will (d) shall

15. (a) lost (b) have lost
(c) am losing (d) was lost

16. (a) would call (b) will call
(c) should call (d) am calling

Directions (Q. Nos. 17-20) Sarita is being interviewed for the job of a teacher in a school. Complete the dialogue by filling in the gaps with thehelp of options given below.

Interviewer : Why do you think you ...**(17)**...

Sarita : Mam, I am qualified for the job and I have a passion for children and teaching. All these traits make me suitable for the job.

Interviewer : Can ...**(18)**... any foreign language?

Sarita : Yes, I can speak and write German.

Interviewer : What ...**(19)**... in graduation?

Sarita : Mam, I have graduated in Chemistry Honours.

Interviewer : Do you ...**(20)**...experience?

Sarita : Yes, I have teaching experience of 5 years in a public school.

Interviewer : Well, then we may consider you for the job.

17. (a) are suitable for the job
(b) is suitable for the job
(c) have been suitable for the job
(d) suitable for the job

18. (a) you able to speak
(b) you spoken
(c) you speak
(d) you be able to speak

19. (a) was your subjects
(b) have been your subjects
(c) had been your subjects
(d) were your subjects

20. (a) have any teaching
(b) have had any teaching
(c) are having teaching
(d) had any teaching

Directions (Q. Nos. 21-24) In the questions given below some situations are given. With help of the options given below choose the correct answer to respond a situation.

21. What do you say when there is a situation which should make you angry but you seem to be calm and feel okay about it? Say, when someone accidentally drops tea on you and apologises.
(a) Watch where you are going!
(b) Are you an idiot?
(c) Its okay. No hard feelings.
(d) I will wash it.

22. What would you say when you have made a mistake, like making multiple errors in an assignment you are supposed to give to your teacher?
(a) I don't generally make mistakes.
(b) I think you can excuse me this time.
(c) I am not an expert you know.
(d) It was so careless of me. I will take care next time.

23. What would you say when you want to ask for help?
(a) I need some help here.
(b) Can anybody help me here?
(c) Could you please help me with this.
(d) Help me with this.

24. How would you decline someone's offer to help you?
(a) Thanks, but I think I can manage.
(b) I am capable of doing this on my own
(c) I don't need your help
(d) Thanks but I don't need it.

Directions (Q. Nos. 25-29) For each of the given sentences, choose the right situation.

25. It is one of the chef's specialities. Its cooked in a microwave with cheese.
(a) Understanding the menu
(b) Complimenting the chef
(c) Welcoming a colleague
(d) going out

26. I am looking for Jama Masjid. Do you know where it is?
(a) At the workplace
(b) At the doctor's
(c) Understanding the map
(d) Fixing an appointment

27. Hello, I would like to change some euros into rupees.

(a) Getting money out.
(b) Asking a friend for money.
(c) Getting change.
(d) Changing currency.

28. Excuse me, could you put your briefcase in the overhead locker?

(a) Getting a taxi. (b) In a hotel suite
(c) In a mall (d) On a plane

29. Leh? It's a wonderful place. Have an amazing time.

(a) Asking for help
(b) asking directions
(c) Wishing for a holiday
(d) Getting information

2 Marks Questions

Directions (Q. Nos. 30-32) From the options, choose the form that best fits the function state to complete the dialogue below.

Rita: Hello, Sita Did you have a good trip?

Sita: It was not too bad. In fact I managed to sleep a bit. ....**(30)**.... .

Rita: Is that all your luggage?

Vicky: Yes. Wait a minute. The small holdall is missing. ....**(31)**.... I must have left it at the duty-free shop.

Rita: ....**(32)**.... We can ask the security guard to get it. Which shop was it?

30. (a) It was so quiet
(b) The passengers slept
(c) The seat was really comfortable
(d) It has made me feel rested

31. (a) Oh dear!
(b) What a nuisance!
(c) Where could it be?
(d) I remember now.

32. (a) Don't cry.
(b) Don't worry.
(c) Are you sure?
(d) We'll look for it.

Direction (Q. Nos. 33-35) Complete the following conversation with the help of options given below.

Wife: If you don't hurry, we'll be late for the show.

Husband: There's a plenty of time. ....**(33)**.... .

Wife: Plenty of time? The show starts in twenty minutes.

Husband: It takes only ten minutes to get there. We can leave now.

Wife: ...**(34)**.... .

Husband: ...**(35)**.... . It's bad for health to be so anxious about everything.

33. (a) Why are you in a hurry?
(b) It's only six o'clock
(c) I won't take long
(d) You are always so impatient

34. (a) Good
(b) That's better
(c) Thank God for that!
(d) It's about time!

35. (a) Slow down
(b) Don't worry
(c) You must be patient
(d) You need to relax a bit more

Directions (Q. Nos. 36-38) Complete the following conversation with the help of options given below

Sonu: Monu, I'm having a get-together in my house on Wednesday night .....**(36)**.....

Monu: I'm sorry Sonu. I won't be able to come. I promised my mother that I will have dinner with her on Wednesday night.

Sonu: ....**(37)**.... How is your mother by the way?

Monu: She's fine, thanks. She often asks me about you.

Sonu: .....**(38)**.....

36. (a) Are you free?
(b) Would you like to come?
(c) I'm sure you'd like to come
(d) If you come, you'll enjoy yourself.

37. (a) Take it easy
(b) You're welcome
(c) That's all right
(d) I don't mind

38. (a) Give her my regards
(b) I hope to see her soon
(c) Tell her that I appreciate it
(d) Tell her that I asked about her too

Directions (Q. Nos. 39-41) Complete the following dialogue by choosing correct options.

Amy: Mother, I have something to tell you.

Mother: What is it?

Amy: .....**(39)**.....

Mother: How did it happen?

Amy: I was dusting the shelf and knocked it over.

Mother: ....**(40)**..... That's the second vase you have broken. I'm going to deduct some money from your allowance each week.

Amy: .....**(41)**..... It was just an accident.

Mother: It'll teach you to be more careful.

39. (a) I didn't finish the dusting
(b) You won't believe what I've done
(c) Promise me you won't get angry
(d) I have broken your favourite vase

40. (a) Not Again!
(b) How could you?
(c) You are really careless
(d) Don't go into my room again

41. (a) Oh no!
(b) That's not fair
(c) I'll complain to father
(d) I don't have enough pocket money

Directions (Q. Nos. 42-44) Complete the following dialogue with the help of options given below.

Rohit: ....**(42)**..... this weekend?

Rajat: I don't have any special plan.

Rohit: How do you like the idea ...**(43)**.... the zoo?

Rajat: That sounds good, But I ....**(44)**.... my parent's permission.

Rohit: I'll come to your house this evening and request your parents to allow you to join me to see the zoo.

42. (a) What are you doing
(b) What will you done
(c) Where were gone
(d) Where did you go

43. (a) in going to
(b) of going to
(c) about the
(d) for gone to

44. (a) Were to take
(b) Were taken
(c) Had taken
(d) need to take

Chapter

16

Verbal Ability

1 Mark Questions

1. Accidents on roads can be prevented, provided the quality of roads is improved and the drivers are instructed in safety rules which they must follow for their own protection. It is also necessary that the illumination on the roads is adequate so as to prevent accidents at night.

This paragraph best supports the statement that

(a) Road accidents are solely due to improper illumination.

(b) Road accidents result in a large number of deaths.

(c) Road accidents are man-made and are always avoidable.

(d) Safety rules are not taught properly to all drivers.

2. The surprisingly abundant life of the Indian Ocean is confined to the upper layers; the deeper and especially the bottom waters are devoid of oxygen and are often permeated with hydrogen sulphide.

The sentence suggests which one of the following:

(a) Observers are surprised at how little life exists in the Indian Ocean.

(b) Hydrogen sulphide is necessary to live.

(c) Both oxygen and hydrogen sulphide are necessary to live.

(d) Oxygen is not necessary for marine life.

3. Many business offices are located in buildings having 2-8 floors. If a building has more than 3 floors, it has a lift. If the above statements are true, which of the following must be true?

(a) Building with 2 floors do not have lifts.

(b) A building having 7 floors has a lift

(c) Only floors above the 3rd floors have lifts.

(d) All floors may be reached by lifts.

4. "Some men are definitely intelligent, others are definitely not intelligent, but of intermediate men, we should say, 'intelligent'? Yes, I think, so or no, I shouldn't be inclined to call him intelligent."

Which of the following reflects the intention of the writer well?

(a) To call men intelligent who are not strikingly so must be to use the concept with undue imprecision.

(b) Every empirical concept has a degree of vagueness.

(c) Calling someone intelligent or not depends upon one's whim.

(d) There is no need to be as indecisive as the writer of the above.

5. Between 1960 and 1970, ivory poachers in the African nation of Zinbaku killed over 6,500 elephants. During that period, the total elephant population in Zinbaku fell from about 35,000 to just under 30,000. In 1970, new anti-poaching measures were implemented in Zinbaku, and between 1970 and 1980 over 800 poachers were arrested and expelled from the country. Nevertheless, by 1980, the elephant population in Zinbaku had fallen to about 21,000.
Which of the following, if true, would best help to explain the apparent paradox presented above?
(a) The poachers arrested in Zinbaku between 1970 and 1980 were rarely sentenced to long prison terms.
(b) Because of highly publicized campaigns against the slaughter of elephants, demand for ivory fell between 1970 and 1980.
(c) The elephant population in neighbouring Membasa rose slightly between 1970 and 1980.
(d) In Zinbaku, between 1970 and 1980, thousands of acres of forest, the elephant's natural habitat, were cleared for farming.

6. If highways were restricted to cars and only those trucks with capacity of less than 8 tons, most of the truck traffic would be forced to run outside highways. Such a reduction in the amount of truck traffic would reduce the risk of collisions on highways.
The conclusion drawn in the Ist sentence depends on which of the following assumptions?
(a) The roads outside highway would be as convenient as highway for most drivers of trucks.
(b) Most of the roads outside highways are not ready to handle truck traffic.
(c) Most trucks that are currently running in highway have a capacity of more than 8 tons.
(d) Cars are at greater risk of being involved in collisions than are trucks.

7. A highly cohesive work group is a prerequisite for high team performance. Sociologists point out that the association between success and group cohesion owes to the support individual team members give to one another and their acceptance of the group's activities and goals.
Each of the following, if true, either supports or cannot weaken the sociologists' assumption about the relationship between success and cohesion EXCEPT
(a) A group of Japanese researchers found that the successful work teams were led by dominant leaders.
(b) University researchers found that there was a significant correlation between team productivity and the extent to which team members understood and complied with the group's objectives.
(c) American researchers found that successful team members tended to rate their fellow members more favourably.
(d) Industrial Psychologists of UK found that work groups who tended to participate in after-hours social activities were more productive.

2 Marks Questions

8. You have made some silly mistakes which have been pointed out to you. You will
   (a) laugh it away
   (b) get angry
   (c) feel miserable
   (d) feel thankful

9. You are moving across the road on a scooter when you observe that two boys on a bike snatch a lady's gold chain and ride away. You would
   (a) Console the woman.
   (b) chase the boys to catch hold of them.
   (c) inform the police about the matter.
   (d) stand and see what happens next.

10. When you see a blind man crossing the road, you
   (a) ask someone to help him
   (b) go and help him
   (c) wait till he crosses the road
   (d) ignore and move on

11. If you are a manager and one of your employees is not working properly, as a manager you would
   (a) fire him.
   (b) give the man two weeks to improve.
   (c) try to develop the man's abilities and interest in another job.
   (d) talk to him and try to find out his problem.

12. A person managing the front office of an organisation should have
   (a) leadership (b) personality
   (c) patience (d) discipline

13. "No risk no gain". You
   (a) feel that risk means no gain.
   (b) believe that this slogan is correct.
   (c) feel it is foolish to accept unnecessary risk.
   (d) feel that risk may be taken only after judging the situation thoroughly.

14. You go to a showroom and like a watch there but it is beyond your budget and is the last of its kind. What do you do?
   (a) You look for similar but a cheaper watch.
   (b) You borrow money from friends.
   (c) You decide that you cannot afford and let it be.
   (d) You come back and after sometime when you have money, try your luck if it is still there.

15. You have gone to enjoy a Diwali Mela organised by a club. Suddenly you come across a lost child crying desperately. You would
   (a) neglect and walk away.
   (b) ask the child to find his parents.
   (c) ask him to stop crying and wait patiently.
   (d) contact with the club authorities and make an announcement for the parents.

PRACTICE SET 01

1 Mark Questions

1. Choose the correct one word substitution for the following.
The practice of having several wives.
(a) Bisexual (b) Monogamy
(c) Bigamy (d) Polygamy

2. Choose the correct meaning of the underlined idiom in the given sentence.
He is selling a new car at a very low price. I <u>smell a rat</u> in this offer.
(a) To suspect foul dealings
(b) A food that tastes bad
(c) To be in a bad mood
(d) To get depressed

3. Change the given sentence from direct to indirect speech.
The little boy said to his father, "Did the Sun rise in the East?"
(a) The little boy asked his father if the Sun rose in the East.
(b) The little boy told his father if the Sun rose in the East.
(c) The little boy asked his father if the Sun rises in the East.
(d) The little boy asked his father if the Sun had risen in the East.

4. Change the given sentence from active to passive voice.
Her selection in the crew surprised Peter.
(a) Her selection in the crew was a big surprise.
(b) Peter was surprised at her selection in the crew.
(c) Her selection was a surprise.
(d) Peter was surprise at her selection of the crew.

5. Replace the underlined word with its correct synonym from the given options. I am trying to <u>abstain</u> from sweets for my new diet.
(a) Arrive
(b) Refrain
(c) Reject
(d) Consume

6. Replace the underlined word with its correct antonym from the given options.
I don't think removing my GPS tracking will <u>dissuade</u> him for long.
(a) Immediate
(b) Rare
(c) Persuade
(d) Tarnish

7. Choose the correct meaning of the underlined idiom in the given sentence.
Rocky is <u>at loggerheads</u> with his brothers because of the property dispute.
(a) To be in extreme danger
(b) To be in love with someone
(c) To be in strong conflict or disagreement with someone
(d) To have a poor memory

8. Change the tense of the given sentence from simple future tense to future perfect tense.
Will I finish writing this book?
(a) Will I has finished writing this book?
(b) Will I have finished writing this book?
(c) Will I has finish writing this book?
(d) Will I have finish writing this book?

9. Change the given sentence from passive to active voice.
The Clean India campaign is being run by the government.
(a) The government was running the Clean India campaign.
(b) The government is running the Clean India campaign.
(c) The government has running the Clean India campaign.
(d) The government has run the Clean India campaign.

10. Choose the correct phrase for the given one word.
Apostate
(a) A person who renounces a religious or political belief or principle.
(b) A person who deliberately sets fire to a building.
(c) A person who does not believe in the existence of God.
(d) A critical judge of any art and craft.

Directions (Q. Nos. 11-15) Fill in the blanks with the correct parts of speech.

11. You were .... than I was but ate .... rice than I did.
(a) more hungry, little
(b) hungrier, more little
(c) hungrier, less
(d) more hungry, less

12. Arjun searched for water .... but he didn't find it ....
(a) everywhere, everywhere
(b) everywhere, anywhere
(c) anywhere, anywhere
(d) anywhere, everywhere

13. He is a difficult .... to talk to sometimes; it is as if I am communicating with a stone ....
(a) person, wall (b) an, glass
(c) person, glass (d) woman, wall

14. Read over your answers .... correct all mistakes before you pass them up.
(a) or (b) and
(c) because (d) while

15. The train was coming .... the station.
(a) back
(b) under
(c) towards
(d) during

16. Change the given sentence from indirect to direct speech.
Ram exclaimed with joy that India had won the World Cup.
(a) Ram said, "India has won the World Cup."
(b) Ram said, "Hurrah! India has won the World Cup."
(c) Ram said, "India won the World Cup."
(d) Ram said, "Hurrah! India had won the World Cup."

17. Change the tense of the given sentence from present perfect tense to past perfect progressive tense.
I have lived in this town for 12 years.
(a) I has been living in this town for 12 years.
(b) I have been living in this town for 12 years.
(c) I had been living in this town for 12 years.
(d) I had lived in this town for 12 years.

18. Fill in the blank with the correct collocations from the given options.
Make sure .... for the test tomorrow.
(a) to have come prepare
(b) to have come prepared
(c) to come prepared
(d) to came prepare

19. Fill in the blank to complete a proper conditional sentence.

.... I have limited money, I always buy the necessary things.

(a) Until (b) Unless
(c) If (d) Since

20. Fill in the blanks with adverbial clause to complete the given sentence.

............, you will not pass.

(a) Unless you work hard
(b) Unless you had worked hard
(c) If you work hard
(d) If you worked hard

21. Replace the underlined word with its antonym to form a proper sentence.

The man had a <u>vindictive</u> streak as wide as the valley, no doubt there.

(a) Graceful (b) Revengeful
(c) Kind (d) Euphoric

22. Rearrange the jumbled parts to form a meaningful sentence.

Oliver Twist/workhouse/in/was/born/a

(a) Oliver Twist in a workhouse was born.
(b) Oliver Twist was born in a workhouse.
(c) Was born Oliver Twist in a workhouse.
(d) Oliver Twist in born was a workhouse.

23. Fill in the blank with the correct collocations from the given options.

He wanted to see if he could .... with us.

(a) got a job (b) get a job
(c) get jobs (d) got jobs

24. Fill in the blanks with noun clause to complete the given sentence.

.... is a genius.

(a) Whoever thought of the idea
(b) However think of the idea
(c) Whenever thought of the idea
(d) Whoever think of the idea

25. Fill in the blanks with a verb in agreement with its subject.

The Committee .... divided on one minor point.

(a) is (b) are
(c) was (d) am

26. Rearrange the jumbled parts to form a meaningful sentence.

Mother Teresa/greatest/missionaries/one of the/was/time/of/our

(a) Mother Teresa was one of the greatest missionaries of our time.
(b) Mother Teresa of our time was one of the greatest missionaries.
(c) Mother Teresa one of the greatest missionaries was of our time.
(d) Of our time Mother Teresa was one of the greatest missionaries.

27. Change the tense of the given sentence from simple past tense to present progressive tense.

We watched a movie in this Cineplex.

(a) We are watching a movie in this Cineplex.
(b) We am watching a movie in this Cineplex.
(c) We have been watching a movie in this Cineplex.
(d) We will be watching a movie in this Cineplex.

28. Fill in the blanks with a verb in agreement with its subject.

Every boy and every girl .... given a packet of sweets.

(a) were (b) are (c) was (d) am

29. Fill in the blank to complete a proper conditional sentence.

.............you .... in this lake, you'll shiver from cold.

(a) If, swam (b) If, swim
(c) Unless, swam (d) Them, swim

30. Change the given sentence from active to passive voice.

Has the company considered your profile?

(a) Has your profile been considered by the company?
(b) Your profile has been considered by the company.
(c) Has your profile considered by the company?
(d) Your profile has considered by the company.

Directions (Q. Nos. 31-35) Read the following passage and answer the questions that follow.

Alfred Hitchcock was a man with vivid imagination, strong creative skills and a passion for life. With his unique style and God-gifted wit he produced and directed some of the most thrilling films that had the audience almost swooning with fright and falling off their seats with laughter. Alfred Hitchcock was greatly influenced by American films and magazines. At the age of 20, he took up a job at the office of Paramount Studio, London. Using imagination, talent and dedication, he made each of his endeavours a success. He took great pleasure in working in the studio and often worked all seven days a week. He moved to the USA in 1939 and got his American citizenship in 1955. Here, he produced many more films and hosted a weekly television show. No matter from where his ideas came, whether a magazine article, a mystery novel or incident, his films had the typical "Hitchcock touch"-where the agony of suspense was relieved by interludes of laughter! Hitchcock was knighted in 1980.

31. What qualities helped Hitchcock achieve success?

(a) His imagination, creativity and passion for life.
(b) His hard work, his imagination and his sense of humour.
(c) His creativity, his passion for life and his sense of humour.
(d) His imagination, his talent and his dedication.

32. What is Alfred Hitchcock famous as?

(a) Writer (b) Film producer
(c) Television actor (d) Film actor

33. What did the typical Hitchcock-style of film-making include?

(a) Fear and passion
(b) Fear and humour
(c) Suspense and humour
(d) Fear and suspense

34. What did Alfred Hitchcock do in United States?

(a) He produced films and read magazines.
(b) He produced films and television serials.
(c) He read magazines and saw films.
(d) He produced films and hosted a television show.

35. What does the word 'swooning' mean?

(a) Fainting
(b) Falling
(c) Hiding
(d) Becoming conscious

36. Fill in the blanks with a verb in agreement with its subject.

Time and tide .... for no man.

(a) wait (b) waits
(c) has wait (d) have wait

37. Change the given sentence from direct to indirect speech.

The police officer said to his team, "Catch the criminal, now."

(a) The police officer said to his team to catch the criminal then.
(b) The police officer ordered his team to catch the criminal then.
(c) The police officer told his team to catch the criminal then.
(d) The police officer advised his team to catch the criminal then.

38. Rearrange the jumbled parts to form a meaningful sentence.

An ant/all through/the summer/wheat/was storing

(a) The summer wheat was storing all through an ant.
(b) An ant was storing wheat all through the summer.
(c) An ant all through the summer was storing wheat.
(d) An ant was storing the summer wheat all through.

39. A part of a notice is given. Read it and answer the question that follow.

The History Association of our school is organising an educational tour to the historical places in Jaipur in the last week of October. The seven day trip will cost ₹ 9000 per person. The charges include bus fare, food and accommodation in a 3 star hotel. Interested students should contact the undersigned latest by 15th October. They are also required to submit a medical fitness certificate and parents' consent letter.

For further information, please contact our administrative office during lunch break or after school hours.

Rahul Goel
President, History Association

What are the children required to submit for the trip?

(a) Bus fare, food and accommodation
(b) Bus fare and medical fitness certificate
(c) Medical fitness certificate and parents' consent letter
(d) Parents' consent letter and accommodation

40. Read the following formal letter and answer the question that follows.

16, Gol Bazar
Yamunanagar
Madhya Pradesh
17th June, 20XX

The Chief Minister
Government of Madhya Pradesh
Bhopal

Subject ....

Respected Sir

This is to bring to your kind notice that five tehsils comprising fourteen villages in the Yamunanagar district are devoid of primary healthcare facilities. Many valuable lives are becoming victims of death everyday due to the insufficiency of hospitals and doctors in our area. There are only two government hospitals in our district.

In case of minor ailments, the poor people have to rely on private clinics in their or nearby villages. But, when there are serious cases or casualties, it is not only very difficult, but also risky to take the patient to the government hospital which is far away from their residence. Even these hospitals are not equipped with adequate facilities. Nor do they have sufficient number of capable doctors. Private hospitals charge very high fees which the poor peasants can't afford.

To check the increasing mortality and deteriorating health conditions in the district, a government hospital with all modern equipment is urgently required. This will cater to the basic needs of healthcare and medicine.

I hope you understand the gravity of the matter and will take necessary steps in this regard as requested.
Thanking you

Yours faithfully
Shalu Mishra

Choose the correct subject for the letter above.

(a) Need for a Government Hospital in Delhi
(b) Urgent Need for a Government Hospital in Yamunanagar
(c) Urgent need for a Pathology centre in Yamunanagar
(d) Urgent for a medical shop in Delhi

2 Marks Questions

41. Match the following.

List I (Idioms)		List II (Meanings)	
A.	To play second fiddle	1.	Perplexed
B.	At one's wits' end	2.	To have a selfish reason for doing something
C.	All in all	3.	Most important
D.	To have an axe to grind	4.	To take a subordinate position to another person

Codes

	A	B	C	D
(a)	1	4	2	3
(b)	4	1	3	2
(c)	3	4	2	1
(d)	2	3	1	4

42. You are returning home from school. On the way, you find a sealed envelope in a street, fully addressed with unused stamps on it. You would:

(a) Remove the stamps and destroy the envelope.
(b) Leave it there as it was and walk away.
(c) Post it at the nearest letter box.
(d) Steal the stamps.

43. Match the following.

List I (One word substitution)		List II (Phrase)	
A.	Agenda	1.	A collection of weapons and military equipment
B.	Arsenal	2.	The points to be discussed at a meeting
C.	Specimen	3.	Something which is used as a sample

Codes

	A	B	C		A	B	C
(a)	1	3	2	(b)	2	1	3
(c)	3	2	1	(d)	2	3	1

44. Complete the following conversation by choosing from the given options.

Sam: Hello Dean, How are you?
Dean: Not so good. I am worried about the coming examination.
Sam: Don't worry.
Dean: I am forgetting everything.
Sam: ....
Dean: I have done well in mathematics but I could not do well in English.

(a) How have you done in mathematics?
(b) When did you do about mathematics?
(c) How did you do about mathematics?
(d) What do you do in mathematics?

Directions (Q. Nos. 45-47) In the following passage, there are blanks each of which has been numbered. Find out the appropriate word from the options in each case.

Around the world, forests are being .... **(45)** ....at a rate of about thirteen million hectares a year and deforestation accounts for an estimated 17% - 20% of all global emissions. In addition, forests and other terrestrial carbon sinks play a ....**(46)**.... role in preventing runaway climate change, soaking up a full 2.6 GT of atmospheric carbon every year. The destruction of forests, therefore, not only emits carbon-a staggering 1.6 GT a year, which severely impairs forests capacity to absorb emissions from other sources-but also drastically ....**(47)**.... the amount of forested land available to act as a carbon sink in the future.

45. (a) Ended (b) Destroyed (c) Extinct (d) Wasted

46. (a) Tough (b) Important (c) Vital (d) Effective

47. (a) Plagues (b) Reduces (c) Shortens (d) Influences

48. If you find yourself in a situation where you are required to make a PowerPoint presentation and you are already bogged down by too much work, as the manager, what would you do?

(a) Cancel the seminar and reschedule according to your convenience.
(b) Take an alternative mode of presentation.
(c) Prioritise your work and try to squeeze out time for it.
(d) Pass the buck to your subordinate as you are the boss and no one can question you.

49. Complete the following conversation and choose from the options given below.

Student: Good morning, sir.
Headmaster: Good morning. What do you want?
Student: Sir, I need a transfer certificate.
Headmaster: ....
Student: You know that my father is a government employee.
Headmaster: Yes. I do.
Student: He has recently got transferred to Chittagong.

(a) Why do you need transfer certificate in the middle of the session?
(b) What do you need transfer?
(c) Who is your father?
(d) Where is your father?

50. An Angry customer wants to meet the senior manager for grievance reporting. What will you do?

(a) Be patient and try to cool him down.
(b) Talk to him yourself and be the fake boss.
(c) Tell him it is not easy to meet the senior manager.
(d) Ask him to leave.

PRACTICE SET 02

1 Mark Questions

1. Choose the correct one word substitution for the following.
The yearly return of a date or an event like a birthday, day of marriage, etc.
(a) Anniversary (b) Ceremony
(c) Annual (d) Recurrence

2. Choose the correct meaning of the underlined idiom in the given sentence.
We had a heavy lunch today, and now I am <u>feeling a bit under the weather</u>.
(a) Being in good health
(b) Not feeling well, or feeling sick
(c) Having energy again after being tired
(d) Doing something that is pointless

3. Change the given sentence from direct to indirect speech.
He said to his father, "I did not go to school yesterday."
(a) He admitted that he had not gone to school the previous day to his father.
(b) He told his father that he had not gone to school the previous day.
(c) He admitted to his father that he had not gone to school the previous day.
(d) He told his father that he would not go to school the previous day.

4. Replace the underlined word with its correct synonym from the given options.
It was a <u>solemn</u> oath of trust that can't be broken.
(a) Spectacular (b) Sincere
(c) Strong (d) Amusing

5. Replace the underlined word with its correct antonym from the given options.
They used to sell useless potions to a <u>gullible</u> public.
(a) Trustful
(b) Stylish
(c) Cynical
(d) Brave

6. Choose the correct meaning of the underlined idiom in the given sentence.
If he doesn't change his behaviour by reasoning, he's going to <u>get a taste of his own medicine</u>.
(a) Believing someone's story without proof even though it may seem unbelievable
(b) Hearing rumors about someone or something
(c) Being treated the way that you have been treating others
(d) To work hard in order to see results

7. Change the given sentence from active to passive voice.
The coach is advising the team about the game plan.
(a) The team advised by the coach, about the game plan.
(b) The team is advised by the coach about the game plan.
(c) The team is given advice by the coach about the game plan.
(d) The team is being advised by the coach about the game plan.

8. Choose the correct phrase for the given one word.

Fatalist

(a) Someone who strictly believes in destiny or fate.
(b) Someone whose age is 100 or more than 100 years.
(c) Someone who is suffering from a fatal disease.
(d) Someone who has woman-like characteristics.

9. Fill in the blank to complete a proper conditional sentence.

.... I reached earlier, I could have caught the train.

(a) Has
(b) Have
(c) Had
(d) Will have

10. Fill in the blank with the correct collocations from the given options.

We need .... for Jim as soon as possible.

(a) find replacement
(b) to find a replacement
(c) to found replacement
(d) found a replacement

Directions (Q. Nos. 11-17) fill in the blanks with the correct parts of speech.

11. He had .... reached the metro station when the metro started.

(a) near (b) fairly
(c) still (d) hardly

12. Mother said to her kids, "Don't go out on a ...., ... day."

(a) sunny, dull
(b) bright, sunny
(c) sunny, bright
(d) dull, sunny

13. I will give you money .... you promise to return it on time.

(a) such that (b) provided that
(c) but (d) and

14. The dog jumped .... the table to catch the mouse.

(a) at (b) in
(c) onto (d) to

15. As a parent, my children's .... is of utmost importance to me.

(a) books (b) wastage
(c) cruelty (d) safety

16. The manager .... the bonus next week.

(a) will gave (b) will give
(c) would gave (d) give

17. .... is the man about whom .... were speaking.

(a) That, we (b) This, I
(c) These, we (d) Those, you

18. Change the given sentence from indirect to direct speech.

Rex ordered his servant to bring him a cup of coffee.

(a) Rex told his servant, "Bring a cup of coffee."
(b) Rex told his servant, "Bring me a cup of coffee."
(c) Rex said to his servant, "Bring me a cup of coffee."
(d) Rex told his servant, "Bring him a cup of coffee."

19. Fill in the blank with the correct collocations from the given options.

Once you get a job, you'll know what .... really is.

(a) hard-earn money
(b) hard-earnt money
(c) money hard-earn
(d) hard-earned money

20. Replace the underlined word with its antonym to form a proper sentence.
Anxiety makes it much harder for a person to <u>articulate</u> their thoughts.

(a) Fluent (b) Eloquent
(c) Volatile (d) Hesitant

21. Rearrange the jumbled parts to form a meaningful sentence.
Spread/healthy carriers/some/of/ diseases/are/germs/by

(a) Some diseases are spread by healthy carriers of germs.
(b) Some diseases are by healthy carriers of germs spread.
(c) Some spread by healthy carriers of germs are diseases.
(d) Some healthy carriers of germs are spread by diseases.

22. Fill in the blank with the correct collocations from the given options.
Could you .... for me?

(a) make reported
(b) made report
(c) do a report
(d) did a report

23. Fill in the blanks with a verb in agreement with its subject.
A plenty of water .... supplied to the villagers.

(a) were (b) are
(c) was (d) has

24. Rearrange the jumbled parts to form a meaningful sentence.
Homophones / are / known as / sounding / words / similar

(a) Similar sounding words are known as homophones.
(b) Homophones are known as similar sounding words.
(c) Similar sounding words are homophones known as.
(d) Similar sounding homophones are known as words.

25. Read the following passage and fill in the blanks with articles.
The Ganga is not merely a river for all .... Indians and more particularly to the Hindus, but it is the lifeline of India and .... physical and spiritual nourisher of crores of its people. It is .... symbol of India's great heritage, ancient traditions, cultures, songs and stories.

(a) a, a, a (b) a, the, a
(c) the, the, a (d) a, the, the

Directions (Q. Nos. 26-30) Read the following passage and answer the questions that follow.

Nepal lies between India and Tibet, among the Himalayan Mountains. The tallest mountain in the world, Mount Everest, is in Nepal, and there are several mountains nearly as high. When mountaineers try to climb Mount Everest, they take the help of the Sherpas, the strong and hardy people who live in these mountains, to carry heavy loads and to act as guides.

A long time ago, the Sherpas crossed over the mountains from Tibet and made their homes along the Southern slopes of the Himalayas in Nepal.

Some Sherpa families have three houses, one house in the lower hills, one a little higher, and one further up. The houses are in small village groups of about forty or fifty. Round each group of houses there are cultivated fields, usually built in the shape of terraces right up the hillsides. In the highest fields the Sherpas grow potatoes; in the lower fields they grow barley; and turnips, garlic and other vegetables in the lower ones. They also graze their yaks on the higher mountain slopes in the summer and on the lower slopes in the winter. Yaks are very hardy, large cattle with thick, hairy blackish-brown coats and long horns. The Sherpas use them for almost everything they need. They ride them, plough with them, and use them to carry their goods. The hairy wool of these animals is made into cloth and their skins into leather boots and tents. The yaks also provide milk, fat and meat. Their dung is dried and used as fuel instead of wood or coal.

26. Where is Nepal situated?
(a) Between Mount Everest and Tibet
(b) Between Tibet and India
(c) Between Tibet and Himalaya
(d) Between Tibet and Mount Everest

27. Sherpas are not known for
(a) their strength and hardness
(b) cunningness
(c) their carrying heavy loads
(d) acting as guides

28. Where do the Sherpas have their houses?
(a) On the lower hills
(b) On a little higher ground
(c) Another a little higher up
(d) All of the above

29. These things Sherpas do not grow on the lower fields:
(a) potatoes
(b) turnip and garlic
(c) other vegetables
(d) barley

30. What are the things for which yaks are not used?
(a) For sports
(b) Wool of these animals is made into cloth
(c) Their skins is made into leather boots and tents
(d) To carry goods

31. Fill in the blanks with a verb in agreement with its subject.
My father in addition to our neighbour............. gone out for a walk.
(a) have (b) has
(c) was (d) is

32. Fill in the blank to complete a proper conditional sentence.
.... I were the president, I would not support war policies.
(a) Then (b) Had
(c) If (d) Has

33. Rearrange the jumbled parts to form a meaningful sentence.
Entertainment / all / become / a great / for / TV / has / source of
(a) TV has a great source become of entertainment for all.
(b) TV has become a great source for all of entertainment.
(c) TV has become a great source of entertainment for all.
(d) Entertainment has become a great source of TV for all.

34. Fill in the blanks with a verb in agreement with its subject.
The furniture in his house .... impressive.
(a) look (b) looks
(c) was looked (d) is looked

35. Change the given sentence from direct to indirect speech.
"Please don't run away", He said.
(a) He said to me please don't run away.
(b) He told me to not to run away.
(c) He begged that I should not run away.
(d) He begged me not to run away.

Directions (Q. Nos. 36-38) In the following passage, there are blanks each of which has been numbered. Find out the appropriate word from the options in each case.

Watermelons came to India during 4th century AD. In the Sushruta Samhita, it is mentioned that watermelons were grown ......**(36)**...... the banks of the river Indus. It was ......**(37)**...... to China during the 10th or 11th century. Wild watermelons are heavier than cultivated ones, some of ......**(38)**...... may weigh up to 20 kg.

36. (a) with (b) in (c) along (d) into

37. (a) bring (b) given (c) took (d) taken

38. (a) it (b) them (c) that (d) few

39. Read the short essay given below and answer the question that follows.

Kashmir is called 'Paradise on Earth'. It is quite unfortunate that this paradise is living in the shadow of terrorism. The peace and tranquility of the valley has been shattered by the acts of terrorism. The valley echoes with the bursts of bullets. Gone are the days when the Dal Lake was overtaken by the inflow of tourists from different parts of the world. Now empty hotels and unoccupied shikaras look towards tourists to occupy them. Tourism in the valley is in shambles. The biggest source of income to the state and the local people has disappeared. The unabated terrorism of the two decades has tarnished the grandeur and glory of Kashmir. Tourism and terrorism can't go together. Law and order must be restored. The youth of Kashmir and other places of tourist interest have the biggest stake to maintain peace and harmony. Local handicrafts and artefacts are in great demand in every part of India. If peace and order is maintained, Kashmir will not take long to attain its old grandeur and glory.

Which of the following can be an accurate title for the essay above?

(a) Shikaras
(b) Kashmiri youth
(c) Tourism and Terrorism in Kashmir
(d) Peace

40. Read the following formal letter given and answer the question that follows.

The Principal,
Aryan Public School,
Paschim Vihar, New Delhi
7th October, 20XX

Subject: ....

Respected sir,

I am Tarun Yadav, studying in Class IX–A of your school. I would like to draw your kind attention towards the problem relateds to our studies. Our Maths and English syllabus have not been completed till now, while half yearly SA-I examination is on head. All students of class IX are facing problems and they are anxious for completing syllabus.

Sir, I request you to arrange extra classes for Mathematics and English as soon as possible so that we can complete our syllabus within time. Sir, please start our classes during recess period. We shall be highly thankful to you for this kindness.

Thanking You
Yours Obediently,
Tarun Yadav

Class IX – A
Roll No – 32

Which of the following is the most accurate subject for the letter above?

(a) Problems of Class IX – A
(b) For starting extra class for Maths and English
(c) Extra class
(d) Complaint of the subject teachers

2 Marks Questions

41. Match the following.

List I (One Word Substitution)	List II (Phrases)
A. Exonerate	1. An imaginary ideal society free of poverty and suffering.
B. Nostalgia	2. Release someone from a duty or obligation.
C. Utopia	3. A sentimental longing or wistful affection for a period in the past.
D. Chronology	4. The arrangement of events or dates in the order of their occurrence.

Codes

	A	B	C	D		A	B	C	D
(a)	1	4	2	3	(b)	4	1	3	2
(c)	3	4	2	1	(d)	2	3	1	4

42. Complete the following conversation by choosing from the given options.

Meenu: Where have you been, Ratna? It's been ages since I have seen you.
Ratna: I had gone to Bengaluru for two months.
Meenu: ....
Ratna: My maternal grandmother.

(a) Whom did you visit in Bengaluru?
(b) Whom have you visited in Bengaluru?
(c) Who are you visiting in Bengaluru?
(d) Whom are you going to visit in Bengaluru?

43. Read the following statements.

If a person is rich, he has a lot of influence.

What influence can you draw from the given statement?

(a) Poor people cannot have influence.
(b) Rama has a lot of influence, so she is rich.
(c) Kamla is rich, so she has a lot of influence.
(d) Gavinda is not rich, so he does not have a lot of influence.

44. Match the following.

List I (Idioms)	List II (Meaning)
A. Bite off more than you can chew	1. To ask the wrong person or follow the wrong course.
B. Barking up the wrong tree	2. To try to do something that is too difficult for you.
C. Handle with kid gloves	3. To be less affected by criticisms and rebuffs.
D. Have a thick skin	4. To treat people with extreme tact and care.

Codes

	A	B	C	D		A	B	C	D
(a)	1	3	2	4	(b)	2	1	4	3
(c)	3	4	2	1	(d)	2	3	1	4

45. Consider the following sentences.

1. A subordinate clause that acts as a noun in a sentence is called a Noun clause.
2. 'The book that you are holding is a masterpiece.' – is an example of noun clause.

Which of these statements is/are correct?

(a) Only 1 (b) Only 2
(c) Both 1 and 2 (d) None of these

46. Match the words given in List I with their synonyms given in List II.

List I	List II
A. Artful	1. Unfeeling
B. Callous	2. Crafty
C. Candid	3. Unfortunate
D. Hapless	4. Blunt

Codes

	A	B	C	D
(a)	2	1	4	3
(b)	4	3	2	1
(c)	1	2	3	4
(d)	2	1	3	4

47. Which of the following sentence(s) is/are grammatically correct and meaningful?

A. You are wasting your's time, the two are incomparable.
B. We lost the first two matches quite baldly.
C. Renu's biting remarks about the newly elected MP left everyone stunned.
D. I scolded my daughter for not completing her homework on time.

(a) A and B
(b) C and D
(c) Only C
(d) Only D

48. Match the words given in List I with their synonyms given in List II.

List I	List II
A. Economise	1. Quiet
B. Bustle	2. Similar
C. Contrary	3. Confirm
D. Nullify	4. Waste

Codes

	A	B	C	D		A	B	C	D
(a)	4	1	3	2	(b)	3	2	4	1
(c)	4	1	2	3	(d)	2	1	3	4

49. Consider the following sentences.

1. An adjective clause is which qualifies a noun or a pronoun in the main clause and does the work of an adjective.
2. It is also known as Relative clause.
3. 'The patient had died before the doctor arrived.' – is an example of adjective clause.

Which of these is/are correct?

(a) 1 and 2
(b) 2 and 3
(c) 1 and 3
(d) None of the above

50. Complete the following conversation by choosing from the given options.

Raju: Do you know that our school is celebrating its golden jubilee next month?

Ravi: Yes, I have heard about it. When is it going to be held?

Raju: It's on the 15th of next month. ....

Ravi: Of course, I will be coming.

(a) You will be coming for it?
(b) Were you coming for it?
(c) You are coming for it?
(d) Will you be attending it?

ANSWERS

Chapter 1 Part of Speech

1. (c) **2.** (d) **3.** (b) **4.** (a) **5.** (c) **6.** (d) **7.** (c) **8.** (d) **9.** (b) **10.** (c)

11. (c) **12.** (c) **13.** (a) **14.** (d) **15.** (c) **16.** (d) **17.** (b) **18.** (c) **19.** (b) **20.** (a)

21. (d) **22.** (d) **23.** (d) **24.** (a) **25.** (c) **26.** (a) **27.** (d) **28.** (c) **29.** (c) **30.** (a)

31. (b) **32.** (d) **33.** (b) **34.** (c) **35.** (a) **36.** (d) **37.** (c) **38.** (b) **39.** (b) **40.** (c)

41. (b) **42.** (b) **43.** (b) **44.** (a) **45.** (a) **46.** (b) **47.** (a) **48.** (c) **49.** (a) **50.** (c)

51. (a) **52.** (c) **53.** (c) **54.** (c) **55.** (b) **56.** (b) **57.** (c) **58.** (b) **59.** (d) **60.** (b)

61. (c) **62.** (b) **63.** (b) **64.** (c) **65.** (b) **66.** (b) **67.** (a) **68.** (b) **69.** (a) **70.** (b)

71. (c) **72.** (c) **73.** (b) **74.** (b) **75.** (c) **76.** (b) **77.** (d) **78.** (a) **79.** (d) **80.** (b)

81. (a) **82.** (a) **83.** (c) **84.** (d) **85.** (d) **86.** (c) **87.** (c) **88.** (a) **89.** (b) **90.** (b)

Chapter 2 Subject-Verb Agreement

1. (b) **2.** (b) **3.** (c) **4.** (a) **5.** (a) **6.** (b) **7.** (b) **8.** (a) **9.** (c) **10.** (d)

11. (a) **12.** (a) **13.** (a) **14.** (d) **15.** (a) **16.** (a) **17.** (a) **18.** (c) **19.** (a) **20.** (a)

21. (b) **22.** (a) **23.** (c) **24.** (b) **25.** (b) **26.** (c) **27.** (a) **28.** (c) **29.** (a) **30.** (b)

31. (b) **32.** (a) **33.** (d) **34.** (b) **35.** (a) **36.** (b) **37.** (c) **38.** (a) **39.** (b) **40.** (d)

41. (b,c,a) **42.** (c,d) **43.** (c) **44.** (d) **45.** (c) **46.** (c) **47.** (d)

Chapter 3 Tenses

1. (a) **2.** (b) **3.** (b) **4.** (b) **5.** (b) **6.** (a) **7.** (b) **8.** (a) **9.** (b) **10.** (c)

11. (a) **12.** (c) **13.** (c) **14.** (c) **15.** (c) **16.** (b) **17.** (c) **18.** (b) **19.** (a) **20.** (b)

21. (c) **22.** (a) **23.** (b) **24.** (c) **25.** (b) **26.** (a) **27.** (c) **28.** (b) **29.** (c) **30.** (c)

31. (b) **32.** (c) **33.** (d) **34.** (d) **35.** (c) **36.** (a) **37.** (a,c,d) **38.** (b,c,d) **39.** (a) **40.** (c)

41. (c) **42.** (b) **43.** (c)

Chapter 4 Clauses and Conditionals

1. (c) **2.** (a) **3.** (c) **4.** (c) **5.** (a) **6.** (c) **7.** (b) **8.** (b) **9.** (c) **10.** (b)

11. (a) **12.** (b) **13.** (d) **14.** (c) **15.** (c) **16.** (a) **17.** (a) **18.** (c) **19.** (b) **20.** (a)

21. (d) **22.** (c) **23.** (d) **24.** (a) **25.** (b) **26.** (a) **27.** (a) **28.** (b) **29.** (c) **30.** (d)

31. (c) **32.** (b) **33.** (b) **34.** (d) **35.** (d)

Chapter 5 Collocations

1. (a)	**2.** (d)	**3.** (a)	**4.** (c)	**5.** (d)	**6.** (c)	**7.** (b)	**8.** (c)	**9.** (a)	**10.** (b)
11. (c)	**12.** (d)	**13.** (a)	**14.** (b)	**15.** (a)	**16.** (c)	**17.** (b)	**18.** (a)	**19.** (c)	**20.** (a)
21. (d)	**22.** (b)	**23.** (c)	**24.** (a)	**25.** (b)					

Chapter 6 Active and Passive Voice

1. (c)	**2.** (a)	**3.** (c)	**4.** (a)	**5.** (b)	**6.** (b)	**7.** (a)	**8.** (a)	**9.** (b)	**10.** (d)
11. (a)	**12.** (b)	**13.** (b)	**14.** (c)	**15.** (a)	**16.** (c)	**17.** (a)	**18.** (b)	**19.** (d)	**20.** (a)
21. (b)	**22.** (d)	**23.** (c)	**24.** (b)	**25.** (a)	**26.** (c)	**27.** (b)	**28.** (c)	**29.** (a)	**30.** (d)
31. (c)	**32.** (d)	**33.** (d)	**34.** (c)	**35.** (c)	**36.** (d)	**37.** (c)	**38.** (a)	**39.** (b)	**40.** (b)
41. (b,a,d)	**42.** (b,a)	**43.** (a)	**44.** (d)	**45.** (c)	**46.** (a)	**47.** (b)	**48.** (b)		

Chapter 7 : Direct and Indirect

1. (c)	**2.** (a)	**3.** (b)	**4.** (b)	**5.** (c)	**6.** (b)	**7.** (b)	**8.** (c)	**9.** (c)	**10.** (c)
11. (c)	**12.** (d)	**13.** (c)	**14.** (b)	**15.** (b)	**16.** (c)	**17.** (c)	**18.** (b)	**19.** (c)	**20.** (a)
21. (c)	**22.** (a)	**23.** (b)	**24.** (b)	**25.** (a)	**26.** (a)	**27.** (a)	**28.** (b)	**29.** (a)	**30.** (c)
31. (b)	**32.** (b)	**33.** (b)	**34.** (b)	**35.** (c)	**36.** (b)	**37.** (b)	**38.** (b)	**39.** (a)	**40.** (a)
41. (d)									

Chapter 8 Jumbled Words/Sentences

1. (d)	**2.** (a)	**3.** (a)	**4.** (d)	**5.** (b)	**6.** (a)	**7.** (d)	**8.** (a)	**9.** (d)	**10.** (c)
11. (d)	**12.** (c)	**13.** (b)	**14.** (c)	**15.** (a)	**16.** (a)	**17.** (b)	**18.** (b)	**19.** (d)	**20.** (d)
21. (c)	**22.** (b)	**23.** (a)	**24.** (b)						

Chapter 9 Synonyms and Antonyms

1. (d)	**2.** (b)	**3.** (a)	**4.** (c)	**5.** (c)	**6.** (b)	**7.** (b)	**8.** (b)	**9.** (b)	**10.** (d)
11. (c)	**12.** (d)	**13.** (c)	**14.** (a)	**15.** (b)	**16.** (d)	**17.** (a)	**18.** (b)	**19.** (b)	**20.** (d)
21. (a)	**22.** (c)	**23.** (d)	**24.** (b)	**25.** (b)	**26.** (a)	**27.** (d)	**28.** (a)	**29.** (c)	**30.** (b)
31. (c)	**32.** (b)	**33.** (a)	**34.** (c)	**35.** (c)	**36.** (a)	**37.** (a)	**38.** (c)	**39.** (a)	**40.** (b)
41. (b)	**42.** (a)	**43.** (d)	**44.** (c)	**45.** (a)	**46.** (c)	**47.** (d)	**48.** (d)	**49.** (b)	**50.** (d)
51. (d)	**52.** (d)								

Chapter 10 One Word Substitution

1. (b)	**2.** (b)	**3.** (b)	**4.** (c)	**5.** (b)	**6.** (a)	**7.** (c)	**8.** (a)	**9.** (a)	**10.** (a)
11. (a)	**12.** (d)	**13.** (a)	**14.** (a)	**15.** (b)	**16.** (b)	**17.** (c)	**18.** (b)	**19.** (a)	**20.** (a)
21. (a)	**22.** (d)	**23.** (b)							

Chapter 11 Idioms and Phrases

1. (c)	**2.** (c)	**3.** (b)	**4.** (b)	**5.** (b)	**6.** (d)	**7.** (b)	**8.** (c)	**9.** (c)	**10.** (b)
11. (b)	**12.** (c)	**13.** (c)	**14.** (d)	**15.** (c)	**16.** (c)	**17.** (c)	**18.** (c)	**19.** (b)	**20.** (b)
21. (c)	**22.** (c)	**23.** (b)	**24.** (c)	**25.** (c)	**26.** (b)	**27.** (a)	**28.** (d)	**29.** (b)	**30.** (a)
31. (b)	**32.** (b)	**33.** (c)	**34.** (b)	**35.** (c)	**36.** (a)	**37.** (c)	**38.** (d)	**39.** (b)	**40.** (b)
41. (c)	**42.** (c)								

Chapter 12 Cloze Test

1. (d)	**2.** (b)	**3.** (d)	**4.** (a)	**5.** (c)	**6.** (d)	**7.** (b)	**8.** (d)	**9.** (b)	**10.** (d)
11. (b)	**12.** (d)	**13.** (c)	**14.** (c)	**15.** (a)	**16.** (d)	**17.** (a)	**18.** (d)	**19.** (b)	**20.** (c)
21. (b)	**22.** (a)								

Chapter 13 Reading Comprehension

1. (b)	**2.** (d)	**3.** (d)	**4.** (c)	**5.** (c)	**6.** (c)	**7.** (c)	**8.** (d)	**9.** (c)	**10.** (c)
11. (a)	**12.** (d)	**13.** (a)	**14.** (b)	**15.** (a)	**16.** (c)	**17.** (b)	**18.** (b)	**19.** (a)	**20.** (c)
21. (b)	**22.** (a)	**23.** (c)	**24.** (b)	**25.** (b)	**26.** (a)	**27.** (c)	**28.** (a)	**29.** (a)	**30.** (b)

Chapter 14 Writing Skills

1. (d)	**2.** (b)	**3.** (a)	**4.** (c)	**5.** (c)	**6.** (a)	**7.** (b)	**8.** (a)	**9.** (b)	**10.** (c)
11. (b)	**12.** (b)	**13.** (c)	**14.** (b)	**15.** (b)	**16.** (a)	**17.** (b)	**18.** (a)	**19.** (b)	**20.** (c)
21. (b)	**22.** (b)	**23.** (a)	**24.** (a)	**25.** (b)	**26.** (b)	**27.** (c)	**28.** (c)	**29.** (b)	**30.** (a)
31. (d)	**32.** (c)	**33.** (c)	**34.** (b)	**35.** (a)	**36.** (c)	**37.** (b)	**38.** (a)	**39.** (a)	**40.** (c)
41. (b)	**42.** (a)	**43.** (c)	**44.** (c)	**45.** (d)	**46.** (a)	**47.** (b)	**48.** (b)	**49.** (c)	**50.** (d)
51. (b)	**52.** (a)	**53.** (a)	**54.** (b)	**55.** (a)					

Chapter 15 Communication Skills

1. (c)	**2.** (b)	**3.** (c)	**4.** (c)	**5.** (b)	**6.** (d)	**7.** (d)	**8.** (c)	**9.** (b)	**10.** (b)
11. (c)	**12.** (c)	**13.** (b)	**14.** (b)	**15.** (b)	**16.** (b)	**17.** (a)	**18.** (c)	**19.** (d)	**20.** (a)
21. (c)	**22.** (d)	**23.** (c)	**24.** (a)	**25.** (b)	**26.** (c)	**27.** (d)	**28.** (d)	**29.** (c)	**30.** (c)
31. (d)	**32.** (b)	**33.** (b)	**34.** (c)	**35.** (c)	**36.** (d)	**37.** (d)	**38.** (a)	**39.** (d)	**40.** (c)
41. (b)	**42.** (a)	**43.** (b)	**44.** (d)						

Chapter 16 Verbal Ability

1. (c)	**2.** (a)	**3.** (b)	**4.** (a)	**5.** (d)	**6.** (c)	**7.** (a)	**8.** (d)	**9.** (b)	**10.** (b)
11. (d)	**12.** (c)	**13.** (d)	**14.** (d)	**15.** (d)					

Practice Set-1

1. (d)	**2.** (a)	**3.** (a)	**4.** (b)	**5.** (b)	**6.** (c)	**7.** (c)	**8.** (b)	**9.** (b)	**10.** (a)
11. (c)	**12.** (b)	**13.** (a)	**14.** (b)	**15.** (c)	**16.** (b)	**17.** (c)	**18.** (c)	**19.** (c)	**20.** (a)
21. (c)	**22.** (b)	**23.** (b)	**24.** (a)	**25.** (b)	**26.** (a)	**27.** (a)	**28.** (c)	**29.** (b)	**30.** (a)
31. (d)	**32.** (b)	**33.** (c)	**34.** (d)	**35.** (a)	**36.** (a)	**37.** (b)	**38.** (b)	**39.** (c)	**40.** (b)
41. (b)	**42.** (c)	**43.** (b)	**44.** (a)	**45.** (b)	**46.** (c)	**47.** (b)	**48.** (c)	**49.** (a)	**50.** (a)

Practice Set-2

1. (a)	**2.** (b)	**3.** (c)	**4.** (b)	**5.** (c)	**6.** (c)	**7.** (d)	**8.** (a)	**9.** (c)	**10.** (b)
11. (d)	**12.** (c)	**13.** (b)	**14.** (c)	**15.** (d)	**16.** (b)	**17.** (a)	**18.** (c)	**19.** (d)	**20.** (d)
21. (a)	**22.** (c)	**23.** (c)	**24.** (a)	**25.** (c)	**26.** (b)	**27.** (b)	**28.** (d)	**29.** (a)	**30.** (a)
31. (b)	**32.** (c)	**33.** (c)	**34.** (b)	**35.** (d)	**36.** (c)	**37.** (d)	**38.** (b)	**39.** (c)	**40.** (b)
41. (d)	**42.** (a)	**43.** (c)	**44.** (b)	**45.** (a)	**46.** (a)	**47.** (b)	**48.** (c)	**49.** (a)	**50.** (d)